A Certain Magni People in the Bedfordshire Landscape

Brian Kerr

A Certain Degree of Magnificence
People in the Bedfordshire Landscape

Brian Kerr

EVENTISPRESS

ISBN 978-0-9932608-6-5

Published in Great Britain in 2018 by Eventispress

Printed by

Print2Demand Ltd

Westoning and Hastings

To my wife, Elizabeth.

Also, to the teachers who made me open my eyes and see the landscape in a different way: Ted Griffiths (Regent House School, Newtownards), Nick Stephens, Jimmy Cruickshank, Rob Glasscock and Robert Common (Queen's University Belfast).

CONTENTS

ACKNOWLEDGEMENTS

Numerous people have actively helped to make this book possible and many others gave active help and encouragement.

The illustration on the front cover is a view of Wrest Park from the terrace of the present house across the French Parterre, planted by the Earl de Grey after the rebuilding of the house in the 1830s. Beyond, the view is dominated by the Long Water (late 1600s) and the Archer Pavilion (early 1700s). The garden and house are open to the public as an English Heritage site. The photograph is by Elizabeth Kerr.

The frontispiece painting is by Californian based artist Jim Trolinger and shows Flitwick Moor, where a bridge crosses the now water filled, former peat diggings. Peat was extracted over several centuries until the mid-1960s, and used locally for fuel and exported to the Midlands. The Moor remains the largest peat deposit in Bedfordshire, and is now designated as a Site of Special Scientific Interest (SSSI).

Images that relate to the excavations at the Black Cat site on the A1 are reproduced here with the kind permission of Archaeological Research Services of Bakewell, Derbyshire. I would like to especially thank Vaughan Dean of Ampthill for the fine photography. Working with the staff at The Higgins Bedford, he created images of implements and objects referred to in the text. The image of the geophysical work at the Old Warden Abbey site was supplied by Margaret Roberts.

Maps and figures were either drawn by John Hambley, while he was based at the Bedfordshire Rural Communities Charity, or by Ian Baillie. Both provided excellent drawings and made helpful suggestions on presentation.

The plan of the possible vineyard in Ampthill was supplied by Andy Chopping of the Museum of London Archaeology from records in the *Northampton Archaeology* journal. Liz Pieksma and Lydia Saul of The Higgins Bedford generously allowed access to the museum's photography collection, and offered abundant contextual information and help. Permission to use images of material from the museum is gratefully acknowledged. I'm also grateful for the help provided by Chris Grabham, Heritage Collection Curator at Luton Culture. Luton Culture kindly gave permission for the use of the paintings by Edward Callam (Figures 5.1b and 12.1).

Figure 4.1, an image of relic medieval ploughing at the village of Littler Staughton, is from a data set of LiDAR imagery for the UK. The copyright is held by the Environment Agency, and use is granted under a Creative Commons Distribution Licence.

Early images of the Firs at Ampthill were supplied by Stephen Hartley. His help in locating the 1918 publication by Herman Porter which records the work of the Canadian Forestry Corps during the Great War is greatly appreciated.

The text has benefited from a professional edit and many people have provided sound advice. Diana Diggins at Eventispress has prepared the manuscript for printing and publication, and has supported, advised and encouraged me throughout the process. Without her support, this book would have never been published.

Given the unstinting help they provided when I wrote my first book, *An Unassuming County: The Making of the Bedfordshire Countryside,* I would have forgiven my friends and family for standing back from a second volume. Despite this, my wife Elizabeth patiently helped to correct this text, and offered practical, well-informed critical suggestions, as did Ian Baillie. Margaret Roberts' diligent editing and comments were especially helpful.

However, I am solely responsible for the content and final presentation of this book. I would be happy to receive comments and corrections: please email wbkerr47@gmail.com.

Brian Kerr   Ampthill, 2018

PREFACE

This book follows my first book, *An Unassuming County: The Making of the Bedfordshire Countryside*. At the heart of this first book was the idea that landscapes and countryside could be explained and understood with a basic knowledge of geology, soils and agriculture. While many people enjoy walking and cycling in the countryside, they may not know much about the history of their local landscape, and I thought this was an opportunity to enhance their pleasure by finding out more about how the landscape was shaped. I wanted to make my account as accessible as possible, avoiding any technical language or complicated geological science.

This book also tries to explain Bedfordshire's modern landscape in a way that is accessible to a wide range of readers.

During 2016, events were held across England to mark the 300th anniversary of the birth of Lancelot 'Capability' Brown. Brown, born in Northumberland in 1716, worked at many sites in Bedfordshire and is often described as 'England's greatest gardener'. The interest surrounding these events raised a number of issues. Why is it that, three hundred years later, we still value and celebrate the landscapes which Capability Brown crafted out of the countryside for the enjoyment of the aristocratic elite? Do we still regard these parkland landscapes, such as the Luton Hoo Estate or Ampthill Park, as typical of the English countryside?

These thoughts led to me writing this book. There is ample evidence that the public care about the landscapes they have access to, and generally value the countryside. While there has been a general loosening of our ties to the land – nine people out of every ten in England now live in an urban location – we still continue to value our countryside, and are protective of it when we perceive it is being threatened. Often these feelings are only expressed when there is a change to the landscape, such as a favourite view is obscured or a well-loved tree removed. There is some irony in the fact that when builders move in to greenfield sites, remove a hedgerow, or fill in a pond, the resulting street of new houses is named Lime Avenue or the Brambles, leaving a memory of the previous countryside. This book was written in a house in such a street – aptly named Fallowfield.

Archaeologists and historians often recognise a number of important themes when studying landscapes and countryside. These apply in Bedfordshire, as in other English counties, and have been explored in this book. For example, many of the landscape features we see are older than we think. It is still possible to identify and appreciate relic features that have not quite been smoothed out of existence by modern farming. A present-day wood may have a distinct boundary ditch, for example, which demarcates the wood as a medieval wood–field boundary, or a hedge line will follow a much older Roman road. A second major theme concerns the continuity in the landscape. The Romans arrived into a largely settled land and then built on top of older Iron Age settlements.

Also, we need to consider the impact of the increasing speed of change as technology provided the tools to make major adjustments to the countryside. Landscaping – as carried out by Capability Brown and the other great gardeners – required many men and many carts, over a long period. Today, the same effect can be achieved in days with modern earth-moving equipment. Finally, there are much more subtle changes we are required to make in land use as the climate changes. This is very much a contemporary theme but there is increasing evidence of earlier warm periods which allowed English vineyards to flourish, as well as – perhaps more significantly – cooler, wetter episodes that had dire consequences for harvests and rural livelihoods.

People play an inescapable part in landscape dynamics. A good example of this in Bedfordshire is the impact of the planting of conifers on less favourable land across the Greensand Ridge during the late eighteenth century. These mostly Scots pine plantations created by the dukes of Bedford have become so familiar today that they are often seen as an intrinsic part of Bedfordshire, and we tend to think of them as the natural land cover. Therefore, at the heart of this account is the realisation that the ideas, energy and, importantly, the wealth of a few individuals are an important driving force to bring about change. Understanding something of the context in which these changes occur, such as the social or agricultural history of an area, enhances our appreciation of what we see in the landscape today.

In preparing this book, I have become aware of the many unnamed and unsung individuals who have played a part in the story of our landscape. While the distinctive work of the illustrious gardeners of the eighteenth century is now rightly celebrated, they were not working on a blank canvas.

In this book I adopt a chronological approach, beginning by unravelling the impacts made on the landscape in prehistory, as people experienced a warming landscape following the retreat of the glaciers. This period brings the challenges of building a landscape picture from archaeological artefacts, residual sites such as Iron Age forts, and increasingly scientific evidence from pollen and pottery. Much later, this account traces the developments in agriculture that took place as farming practices and landscapes changed to embrace steam and later diesel power. Finally, the book looks briefly to the future, at changing public perceptions of the countryside and what it is for.

In taking this landscape history approach, I acknowledge the influence of others who have followed this familiar theme, notably the pioneering work of W.G. Hoskins in his masterly book *The Making of the English Landscape*, published in 1955. Others have charted the evolution of the Bedfordshire landscape, such as Peter Bigmore in *The Bedfordshire and Huntingdonshire Landscape* (1979). Simon Houfe took a more orthodox historical approach in his book *Bedfordshire* (1995), and Joyce Godber wrote the comprehensive *History of Bedfordshire* (1984).

This more modest account complements these detailed histories by placing changes to the land at the centre of the story, at the same time recognising and celebrating the people who had the energy, vision and money to effect change.

Whatever the mix of influences, we have inherited a countryside that is distinctive, interesting, appreciated, even loved, by many. This brings us back to 'England's greatest gardener' and the garden landscape movement that so influenced not only the actual landscape but also how we think an English landscape should look. While Capability Brown (1716–83) grabs all the attention, many landowners later turned to Humphry Repton (1752–1818), who worked for the 'new money' coming into the countryside and sold 'ideas', rather like a modern consultant or designer. His approach had practical appeal to landowners, and he was often successful at selling his plans to the lady of the household. His designs emphasised economy, convenience and what he termed 'a certain degree of magnificence'. I have borrowed Repton's phrase for the title of this book.

One aim of this book is to highlight trends in agriculture and land use, and the significant changes which have had an effect nationally – and indeed globally – but which have left traces in the local landscapes we see today. Where possible, I have acknowledged individuals or elites who embodied these changes and left a mark or imprint on the English countryside. The Norman elite, who introduced rabbits, left a legacy of warrens on the Greensand Ridge, for example, as did the army of drainers, mainly Irish, who transformed much of the extensive clay land of Bedfordshire into productive grain fields. All have played a part in shaping the present-day countryside.

Since the publication of *An Unassuming County* in 2014, I have become increasingly aware that many people have a real and significant interest in the modern countryside and how it is used today. Furthermore, people are interested in the people who have undertaken or inspired these major historical countryside changes – hence the national interest in Capability Brown. Local histories and stories resonate with any audience who can readily grasp the significance of land and how it has been used in the past. In this book, my focus on local, not national, events allows history to be viewed in an immediate, relevant and new light. While most people have some understanding of the larger picture of British history, such as the Norman invasion of England, the importance of the motte and bailey castles throughout Bedfordshire, and how we can learn about the settlement of the county from the later Domesday record, is often overlooked. Therefore my challenge was to relate national environmental, social and economic changes to one small county in the middle of England.

At this point it is important to mention what the book does not try to do. It is far from an academic history of Bedfordshire. It does not spend a lot of time discussing the governance of the county. This is not the place to look for an account of the owners or builders of the great houses, nor the lives of military men, politicians or statesmen from Bedfordshire. The parkland estates and country houses do figure in this book, but it is not about garden history or architectural history. Additionally, while this book traces the changes that have taken place in agriculture, it is not intended as an economic history or an accurate account of land ownership. That is not the aim.

Rather, this second book has a simple objective: to encourage more people to visit, and enjoy, the countryside; perhaps to discover some of Repton's 'magnificence'; and at the same time to begin asking questions about the landscape. Despite farm open days and television programmes such as *Countryfile*, the daily work of the countryside manager, farmer, forester or gamekeeper is still something of a mystery to the average person. Modern agriculture is as dependent on GPS satellite receivers as it is on silage making. Hopefully this book will appeal to an audience that is curious about what they see when outdoors.

This curiosity is important, as the speed of change is now rapid. European farm policy over the past two decades has impacted on both the crops grown in the UK and environmental regulations, which have encouraged conservation. At the same time, there are less obvious changes, such as ash dieback in British woods and a marked decline in farmland birds, such as the lapwing. Therefore an informed curiosity which encourages us to understand how the present landscape evolved will be necessary in shaping new directions. The better we understand how the present landscape evolved, the more we can influence new directions it will take. The challenge in the face of mounting pressures on land is to conserve the best, and most diverse, of what we have. To achieve this, we must understand as much as we can, and learn quickly, since government policy on the countryside is likely to figure prominently in public debate over the next few years. It would be surprising if the imminent removal of the annual £3 billion European subsidy had no impact. Is this an opportunity to do things differently?

Finally, a few brief notes on the structure of this book. It takes a straightforward chronological approach, beginning with humans arriving from Europe after the ice retreated and the land had begun to warm. The following chapters pick out fundamental changes in the landscape and set these within the historical narrative. However, the weakness of this approach is that the time periods do not fall into neat slots. The influence of the Romans in southern England carried on long after the departure of the military garrison, and the period of enclosure, which gave us the present-day field pattern, was also the era of innovative garden and landscape design. Imposing a rigid framework of dates does not do justice to these overlapping trends. Therefore dates have been added where appropriate and where there is an accepted historical record, but defining the chapters solely by dates has been avoided where possible. I have used the well understood AD and BC nomenclature. Similarly with historic measures of area, I have retained the use of acres; only when there is a direct modern quote have I used hectares.

A location sketch map (Figure P.1) has been added to assist the reader. A timeline (Figure P.2) has also been included, to give the historical context. For brevity, Bedfordshire's major river, the Great Ouse, is often foreshortened to the Ouse. In a similar way, the Higgins Art Gallery and Museum, a Bedford institution often described locally as 'the museum' or 'the art gallery', is referred to in the text as The Higgins Bedford. The geographic area described is confined largely to Bedfordshire, with occasional excursions into neighbouring counties to make a specific point.

Joyce Godber explains that not until 1011 was the word 'Bedfordshire' used in the *Anglo-Saxon Chronicle*. Therefore, while the chapters dealing with the period prior to the Norman invasion use the county name, they are referring to the general area that is now Bedfordshire. The Roman garrison would not have recognised Bedfordshire as a place name.

All the sources I consulted while writing this book are listed in the Further Reading section. I have also listed a selection of the stately homes, nature reserves and historic sites mentioned in this book in the Appendix. This is not an exhaustive list but is intended to provide a flavour of the Bedfordshire countryside. Many locations have websites that provide more information; others will require a map and a sense of adventure to locate.

Brian Kerr   Ampthill, Bedfordshire, 2018

Places mentioned in text

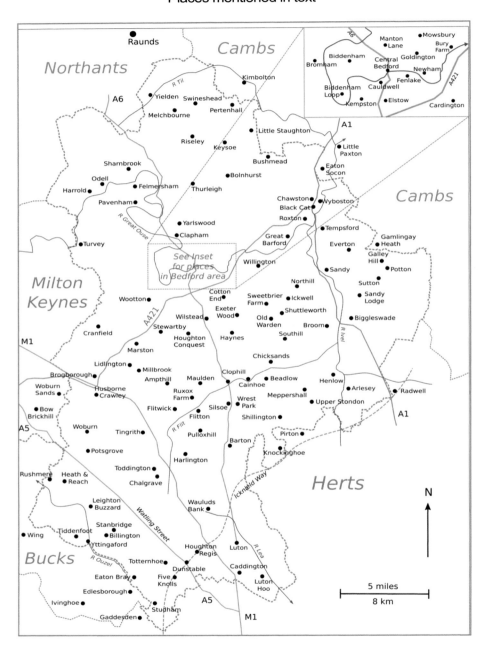

(Figure P1)

Timeline for the agricultural landscape of Bedfordshire

Chapter	Approximate dates	Cooler or warmer than 1900	National events	Bedfordshire examples
1 A Warming Land	ca 10500 - ca 2500 BC	Glacial retreat	Stonehenge	Biddenham Loop camps Palaeolithic implements in clay pits
2 A Settled Land	ca 2500 BC - 43 AD		Maiden Castle fort Celtic fields	Hill forts at Mowsbury & Sandy Iron Age finds at Stewartby
3 Roman Farms and Farmers	43 - 410	Vineyards	Roman arrival Departure of Roman garrisons	Romano-British farms at Priory Park Manton Lane villa
4 New Arrivals	410 - 1066		Saxon kingdoms Viking/Danish raids	Saxon town at Kempston Bedford retaken (915)
5 The Campaign for Information	1066 - ca 1300	Medieval Warming	Domesday Book (1086) Open field agriculture	Local mottes Bedford, Cainhoe, Ampthill Castles
6 Things Fall Apart	ca 1300 - ca 1700	Little Ice Age	Black Death reaches London (1348) Dissolution of monastries (1535-1550)	54 priests die in Bedfordhsire (1349) Warden Abbey (1537)
7 & 8 Gardens, Parks and Farms	ca 1700 - ca 1850		Enclosure Acts Repton & Capability Brown gardens & parks	Felmersham Enclosure Act (1765) Woburn, Wrest Park, Southill, Luton Hoo
9 High Farming	ca 1850 - 1914		Corn Laws repealed (1846) Steam plough	Howard plough Foundation of Britannia Iron Works
10 Ploughing Up	1914 - 1946		War years Grassland converted to arable	Country houses, e.g. Wrest Park, used in war effort
11 Finding a Balance	1946 - Present		EU Common Agricultural Policy Planning, Access & Conservation Acts	Last bricks made (2008) Marston Vale Forest (1991)
12 Preachers, Painters and Poets	Post -1600		Social reformers, Howard & Wilberforce, have Bedford connections	Bunyan imprisoned (1660-1672) Edward Callam paintings 1930s
13 The Power of Place	Post - 2019	Global warming	National agricultural & countryside plans Post-Brexit	Cambridge-Oxford corridor New towns proposed

(Figure P2)

CHAPTER 1
A WARMING LAND – HUMAN FOOTPRINTS
(10,500–2500 BC)

'When a clearing is made, something profound has happened: the land has been worked, it has been invested in, and a sense of possession begins to take shape.'
Garrett Carr (*The Rule of the Land*, 2017, p. 248)

There is no clear starting place for this account since, prior to recoded history, all evidence of how people made use of their natural resources depends on the interpretation of archaeological excavations and the artefacts recovered. While the number of excavations taking place has increased, and this is now a mandatory requirement prior to any development that disturbs the land, constructing an accurate picture of landscape change is still based on a limited number of finds and excavated sites across this area of southern England. Also, interpretation of the evidence found is subjective, and trends and fashions in archaeology are as fickle as in other disciplines. However, three threads are consistent in this story: (1) the earliest date for which there is evidence of people interacting with the land is continually being pushed back, making the account of human occupation older than we think. While Britain has been populated for hundreds of thousands of years, the arrival of farmers who shaped the land started the process of landscape change; (2) a warming climate following the retreat of the ice, which can be approximately dated to 15,000 years Before the Present (BP), encouraged settlement, and people began to change the landscape in southern England; and (3) most people came from continental Europe, entering Britain either along the major rivers or along the drier chalk downs. Bedfordshire was an important route into middle England.

The title of this chapter was carefully chosen to reflect the start of a continuous occupation of southern England as the ice sheets retreated. However, the exact chronology of the multiple ice advances across lowland England is still a matter of discussion among geologists and archaeologists, and the dates adopted in this book refer to when southern Britain began to warm. Geologists refer to this as the Holocene. It began around 12,000 BP.[1] This is only a fleeting time span within the much longer Pleistocene, which began in northern Europe about 2.6 million years ago.

During this time, fluctuations in global temperature led to several advances of ice into southern England. The most significant ice advance was the Anglian glaciation, during which ice ground a path from Scandinavia across the North Sea and into the chalk lands of Norfolk and Cambridgeshire, eventually reaching the edge of the Chilterns in Bedfordshire. During this period Britain was not an island but a peninsula of the north-west European continent, with access across the North Sea via a now submerged land bridge known as Doggerland. (This is the origin of the name of the sea area, familiar from the shipping forecast.) The land bridge provided a level, if boggy, entry point into lowland Britain for migrating people, plants and animals.

In May 2013, fossilised human footprints were found in a newly uncovered sediment layer on a beach at Happisburgh in Norfolk: they have been dated to around 800,000 BP, making them the oldest known hominid footprints outside Africa. These early people are thought to have crossed the land bridge via the Doggerland terrain and entered what we now call East Anglia and Lincolnshire. Geologists believe these early settlers were then driven out of Britain by the increasing cold, which peaked in the later extensive Anglian ice advance across Bedfordshire.

These glaciers gouged and scraped out large volumes of clay-rich sediments, which the ice transported across the landscape and deposited as spreads of chalk-rich glacial till or sticky boulder clay. This has become the most common subsoil in Bedfordshire, familiar to any arable farmer or a winter walker crossing ploughed land. This clay-rich deposit is characteristic of the uplands across north Bedfordshire: this exposed, relatively high land without much shelter makes this a colder landscape for arable farming, with crops here being harvested later than south of the River Ouse. These deposits are from two distinct episodes representing the fluctuations of the Anglian ice margin which, geologists agree, came to abut the edge of the Chilterns, leaving only the highest hills on the chalk escarpment free of ice.

---

[1] Dates in these early chapters refer to time Before the Present (BP). When historical sources are available in the later chapters, the dates used are AD and BC.

Bedfordshire and Hertfordshire were probably only glaciated once during the Anglian advance, but a subsequent cold period brought Arctic conditions to all of southern England, which repeatedly modified the landscape. The later ice advance to the English Midlands (during what is known as the Devensian cold phase) brought the ice front south to what is often called the Wolverhampton line. South of this ice limit the climate was characterised by geologists as a 'periglacial environment', with the land frozen to some 10 metres (32 feet) below the surface. This period also altered the landscape, with large volumes of water carving out and widening valleys across the Bedfordshire Chalk and Greensand Ridge. One result of this cold climate was the deposition of loess, a fine-grained, windblown material made up of fine silt and clay particles, south of the ice front. These localised clay deposits were later important for local brick-making – and, during small-scale clay extraction, the earliest manmade tools in this area were unearthed.

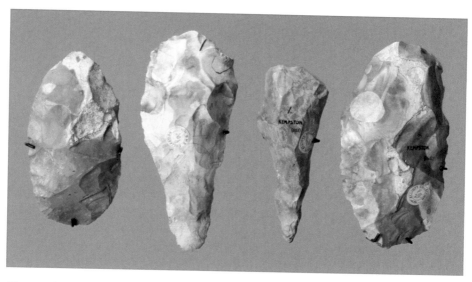

Figure 1.1. Palaeolithic hand axes. In Bedfordshire Palaeolithic hand axes were usually made of flint and recovered from sands and gravels deposited by glacial rivers. They varied in age from 350,000 to 50,000 BP. These examples are from Biddenham and Kempston. (Image by Vaughan Deane from a collection in The Higgins Bedford.)

In Bedfordshire, places such as Caddington and Gaddesdon Row on the southern (or dip) slope of the chalk became nationally important archaeological sites where many stone tools were discovered (Figure 1.1). The first appearance of artefacts created for use by humans in Britain is called the Palaeolithic period. It lasted from the first appearance of artefacts to the end of the last ice age. Dating these deposits in which the tools were found has been a challenge for archaeologists, who have concluded that these areas were occupied during periods of warming within these earlier glacial episodes.

Figure 1.2. Worthington Smith in a gravel pit. Worthington George Smith was a Victorian collector of antiquarian finds in Bedfordshire. He collected and classified manmade tools from both clay and gravel workings. Many of these are in the Wardown Park Museum, Luton. (Image courtesy of Luton Culture.)

A Dunstable historian, Worthington George Smith (1835–1917) (Figure 1.2), collected and described archaeological artefacts from many Bedfordshire sites after he realised the clay pits were yielding manmade flint implements. He then painstakingly recorded these finds. In 1890 he documented large numbers of flint tools from a site at Caddington, and later realised he had discovered an important Stone Age working site where stone implements had been produced on a considerable scale. Almost a ton of these were collected over the next few years as the clay pits were extended: the best of these are now preserved in the British Museum in London. Further investigations were carried out in 1970–71. They confirmed Smith's conclusion that this was a significant Palaeolithic site and also recovered remains of mammoth, rhinoceros and deer. The site at Caddington was either a flint tool manufacturing site or a temporary camp used during a warm interlude between the major ice advances.

Other finds surfaced from the sand and gravel workings at Biddenham, where the ancestral River Ouse once meandered across a wide floodplain. This would have been an attractive site for humans and animals to come into contact: artefacts recovered here include flint tools and an array of bones from now extinct mammals. Dating this collection of finds is difficult, but archaeologists believe this site was utilised during one of the warmer periods of the last ice age when the ice retreated, to allow both plants and animals to become established in southern England. The Biddenham site (findings from which were recorded by eminent Bedford antiquarian, James Watt, in 1861) is important because the flint axe heads retrieved from the site provide a connection linking Palaeolithic man as a tool-maker and animals that are now extinct.

The dating of glacial episodes such as the Devensian ice advance is imprecise, but it is agreed that the maximum cold period was likely between 27,000 and 20,000 BP, and that by 12,500 BP the climate in southern Britain was warming. The retreat of the final ice advance also marked the submergence of the North Sea land bridge, known as Doggerland, which had provided a route into Britain. Birch trees and grass began to colonise the landscape, and summer temperatures would have reached the around 17°C. However, this was not an uninterrupted warming; scientists have noted a return to cold conditions around 8000 BP. Later pine and alder forests became common and the open landscape began to disappear. Man hunted wild boar, pig and wild cattle across this warming land. Detailed archaeological excavations are important to establish how the land was used. An example is the excavations within the Biddenham Loop before the land was developed for housing. Over 100 Palaeolithic hand axes were unearthed here, suggesting possible trading.

The Biddenham Loop

An ideal place to live?

Excavations in advance of the housing development within the meander of the River Great Ouse (Figure 1.3) led to a remarkable history of occupation and settlement being unearthed, from the discovery of Palaeolithic hand axes to Roman pottery. The findings have been published in two books by Albion Archaeology – *Life in the Loop* (2008) and *Close to the Loop* (2016).

The senior author, Mike Luke, brings together a group of specialists to unravel this history, beginning with some 100 hand axes which may have been moved by the river and are therefore undated. A later occupation in the Mesolithic period has been also noted, marked by the spread of flint tools. This riverside location would have been favoured by hunter-gatherers utilising the river for fishing and the nearby woodland for hunting. The first pottery – coarse clay vessels commonly known as Peterborough ware – marks the occupation of the river terraces by more settled communities that were raising domesticated animals and perhaps cultivating grain. These finds have been dated from 3500 BP to 2700 BP.

The first metalworking evidence from these sites includes a dress pin, and there are indications that pits were aligned across the site to define a settled area, which in the Iron Age become four distinct farms with storage pits and domesticated animals. Grain was being ground into course flour on-site using quern stones (see Chapter 2). Later in the Iron Age the farming expanded further, with additional enclosures (defined by ditches), pottery and identifiable house sites.

Romano-British settlement meant more farmsteads, which were linked by tracks across marshy ground. Imported Roman pottery also points to a continued contact with Europe. This was clearly a mixed farming community, settled within a defined boundary.

During the Mesolithic period, flint tools became more sophisticated, and flint blades were carried from place to place by hunters or perhaps traded into areas that had limited usable flint resources. For example, notable collections of flint tools have been found in the central part of the Greensand Ridge, where large natural flint nodules are rare. Heathland at Sandy and in Ampthill Park has yielded large numbers of flint scrapers and some fine arrowheads.

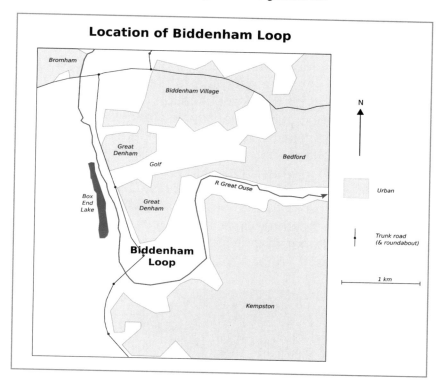

Figure 1.3. The location of the Biddenham Loop.

There are a number of reasons why early people would have wanted to change the landscape. Regular burning of grasslands when dry would encourage new growth, tempting animals such as deer to graze in larger numbers, and people would then hunt these animals. The evidence for the exact methods used by the hunters is uncertain, but it is clear that fire was one of the first elements used to make a significant impact to habitats.

These early inhabitants of lowland England were highly mobile and carried toolkits of blades and other flint implements to fashion tools. The items retrieved close to Priestley Farm at Flitwick included a large number of Mesolithic blades and smaller cutting tools known as microliths. The diverse range of tools suggests this may have been a site where tools were made. The siting of these finds on a river terrace is important: people living in a subsistence economy would have made use of the wet land by the river and the woodland on the dry slopes. It is clear that people in these societies were knowledgeable about the available natural resources and chose working and settlement sites to maximise the range of opportunities offered by the landscape.

As the need for a more sustainable food supply began to put pressure on local environments, the hunter-gatherer way of life was slowly replaced by the domestication of crops, and the first signs of farming became evident in lowland England. Recent excavations on the Isle of Wight have evidenced wheat grains impressed into pottery, dating to around 5000 BP. This was a foretaste of farming in what is called the Neolithic period, requiring more sophisticated implements and tools. The appearance of pottery and rather beautiful leaf-shaped arrowheads and polished axes happened at the same time that people established distinct, settled territories rather than living a nomadic existence, as they had in earlier times.

Figure 1.4. Neolithic hand axes. By 6000 to 4300 BP, Neolithic tools (as illustrated here) reflected early humans' more settled life. These hand axes would have been used to clear land for farming. They are from excavations at Burnt Fen (Cambridgeshire) and Stotfold (Bedfordshire). (Image by Vaughan Deane from a collection in The Higgins Bedford.)

Archaeologists have concentrated on the technological changes taking place in the tools and monuments at the beginning of the Neolithic period. However, perhaps the most profound impact was when man began to clear land for farming, however small and piecemeal the scale. The quote at the beginning of this chapter captures the significance of this act of deliberately changing how the land is used. As the author, Garrett Carr, explains in *The Rule of the Land* in a discussion on early farming in Ireland, Neolithic farmers now had axes in their hands – and so land clearance began: 'When a clearing is made something profound has happened: the land has been worked, it has been invested in, and a sense of procession begins to take shape.' Other advances follow – domestication of animals, sowing crops and building permanent structures. All of this means commitment to a specific area: a process that transforms into territory' (p. 248).

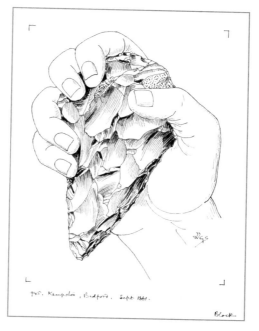

Figure 1.5. A drawing of the Kempston axe being held. Worthington George Smith was a talented artist, and this fine line drawing shows how the Palaeolithic tool would fit comfortably in a hand. The implement was excavated from Kempston. (Image from the Luton Museum collection.)

Clearing land requires effort and some co-operative organisation, many hard-won tools, and time. Archaeologists have experimented with replicas of these Neolithic axes and managed to fell an oak tree in one day of hard labour (Figures 1.4 and 1.5). The natural extension of clearing land is that it will require a boundary and markers to demarcate entitlement. In some places in Ireland, these are still visible, and common. They signal the beginnings of human settlement.

The question that has not yet been answered is: how much of this transition came about by the indigenous population adopting new ideas, and how much by continental incomers filling the gaps in the British landscape? There was once a wide acceptance that the Neolithic or First Agricultural Revolution marked a significant transition from a period of hunting and gathering to a more settled lifestyle based on farming, which made an expanded population possible, but the degree of overlap is uncertain. What has been agreed, however, is that humans were already having a measurable impact on the environment. The study of pollen in peat deposits is an established science, and there are strong indications that woodland was giving way to open grassland during this period, when weeds associated with agriculture begin to appear. Forest clearance was required for the production of cereal crops such as wheat and barley, and sheep and goats were new additions to the native pigs and cattle.

In Bedfordshire, earthworks from this archaeological period were mostly connected to communal meeting areas or burial sites. In other areas of Britain with favourable hard rock geology, stone-built houses were common, and in wetter parts of Britain such as the Cambridgeshire Fens and Somerset Levels, wooden tracks are indications of occupancy. In this part of lowland Britain, the monuments are less visually impressive. By the late Neolithic (around 2500 BP), 'henge monuments' were being built, reaching a climax with Stonehenge. There is a less well-known henge structure at Wauluds Bank in the Lea Valley, close to the source of the river, where many Neolithic arrowheads have been found. The value of carrying out archaeological explorations ahead of any land disturbance is shown by the find of a Neolithic cursus (or ritual site) that was exposed when the Biggleswade sewage plant was being extended. Another example is the hill fort now perched close to the edge of a chalk quarry at Maiden Bower. The proximity of the Icknield Way, which is within a mile of this site, raises the question of how old these ancient routes are. Since this elevated, dry route for travellers can be traced from Dorset to the north Norfolk coast, it is reasonable to suggest it may have been in use at the very beginning of the Bronze Age. However, this is still open to debate.

It is clear is that favoured sites for settlement in Bedfordshire included the better-drained gravel terraces of major rivers such as the Ouse and the Ivel, as well as the dry chalk uplands. The opening of sand and gravel workings along the Ouse has uncovered other sites of Neolithic settlement, including at Little Paxton in Cambridgeshire and along the river terraces at Cardington, close to Bedford. An interesting example came from the site of what is now the Tesco store on Goldington Road to the east of Bedford: a multi-phase Neolithic/Early Bronze Age circular enclosure (and later barrow) at Bury Farm was excavated in 1987, in advance of housing development. The site had previously been recorded as a crop mark only. (A crop mark is a pattern that is visible in growing crops at certain times of the year.) However, excavations revealed a double ring ditch and later Bronze Age burials. The provisional sequence of development suggested an early Neolithic phase, with an enclosure ditch and perhaps a henge monument, together with a number of small pits that contained deposits including hazelnuts, broken fragments of pots known as potsherds, grinding stones known as querns (used to remove the outer husk of grain), and part of a polished flint axe. The later phase showed that settlement continued there into the Bronze Age, with two crouched burials found in separate pits, as well as a small pottery vessel.

Therefore, the population was increasing as the climate warmed, the clearance of land was under way on both the gravels and the chalk, and the movement of people through Bedfordshire into the heart of England using the Icknield Way was established. These trends were to continue, and accelerate, as metal tools replaced stone. The Neolithic period moved into the Bronze Age, when metal tools were used, which led to improved cutting tools, including iron-tipped ploughs, later in the Iron Age.

CHAPTER 2
A SETTLED LAND (2500 BC–AD 43)

The archaeological landscape of Bedfordshire does not have the immediate visual impact of areas such as Wessex, with burial mounds scattered across the chalk uplands, nor does it benefit from the imposing stone-built structures that enrich the landscape of northern and western Britain. The archaeologist in this corner of England needs to create a prehistory with trowel, spade and patient excavation. Generally we are not very good at the appreciation of prehistory; we like our history to begin with the Romans, who built things that are tangible, and helpfully wrote things down. However, one advantage of today's housing and infrastructural building boom across Bedfordshire is that archaeological investigation is now mandatory prior to any building development, and the skill of the 'rescue diggers', in advance of the bulldozers, has added greatly to our understanding of prehistory. This growing volume of excavation information is gradually being linked, with the help of digital mapping, to create a spatial picture of what the prehistoric landscape may have looked like. Modern archaeology, which incorporates scientific techniques such as the mapping of structures with geophysical probes, and employs high-powered microscopes to study seeds and pollen grains, is now offering greater insights into time periods prior to recorded history. These new findings can be fitted into a story or framework which will stand up to scrutiny until a new theory emerges.

This type of evidence in general supports the understanding that, equipped with metal tools, early settlers began to clear land beyond the previously favoured areas of the chalk and moved on to the flat river terraces. The importance of this underlying geology and the soils derived from this is fully explored in *An Unassuming County: The Making of the Bedfordshire Countryside*. The soil cover on the open chalk downlands was thin, the land was sloping, but at the same time the population was growing, and so was the demand for cereals. Land was becoming a valued resource.

There is broad agreement on indicators marking the end of the Neolithic period at around 2500 BC in Britain. First, a number of changes in pottery types; second, the emergence of metal artefacts; third, the abandonment of earlier communal monuments, such as Stonehenge, and an increased emphasis on individual burials. Archaeologists can now recognise a 'package' of cultural traits which were rapidly spreading across lowland England. These included copper and later bronze implements – and the new technology to produce them. The age of the metal worker had arrived.

However, in Bedfordshire this period has much in common with the preceding Neolithic, and the continuity of settlement was as important as the new practices. An example is the abandonment of the Neolithic henge monument at Wauluds Bank in the Lea Valley, north of Luton, and its later reoccupation in the Iron Age, after a break of around 1500 years.

The Bronze Age: more than just the barrows

As it has in much of lowland England, the study of this period of prehistory has been dominated by the excavation and interpretation of burial monuments, often referred to as 'barrows', in areas south of the Thames. Excavation in the 1930s at the Bronze Age site at Five Knolls on the edge of the Dunstable Downs revealed a round barrow cemetery with cremated remains typical of other Bronze Age sites, together with an earlier – perhaps Neolithic – burial, again underlining the continuous occupation of preferred locations. More recent investigations of Bronze Age sites in Bedfordshire have been limited to crop marks appearing in arable fields, which often mark a former ring ditch, now infilled. The majority of these trace sites are on the Great Ouse and Ivel gravel terraces, with around twenty-five identified in this part of Bedfordshire and only a handful elsewhere in the country. The absence of evidence of barrows suggests that the Greensand Ridge may still have supported considerable areas of woodland in the Bronze Age period. This distribution of sites along the major river valleys supports the idea that settlement was becoming common here, and some form of agriculture was being undertaken. Future excavations may reveal more evidence of livelihoods based on farming. This is a shift in archaeological thinking, requiring detailed work on less visually impressive sites rather than the more obvious field monuments.

Bronze is a much harder metal than copper but is still relatively easily worked, requiring the addition of small amounts of tin to the copper alloy. The metal was used for decorative work, and gradually replaced the early flint tools such as the hand axe. Bronze Age finds of such tools keep appearing, such as the axe head from an unknown site in Bedfordshire which was offered on eBay in February 2017 for the bargain price of £275. There are also archaeological records of two socketed axe heads from Bromham, and burial sites at Roxton and Willington.

There is now a consensus that this was the period when farming really accelerated, following significant woodland clearance in the Neolithic period. While communities may still have depended on itinerant flocks and herds, cultivation demands a more settled presence – to water, weed and harvest crops. With the advent of metal working the clearance was stepped up, and organised field systems began to emerge as a response to an increasing population. The landscape was filling up with people, livestock and crops: boundaries of some sort became necessary. The current understanding is that landscapes previously referred to by archaeologists as 'celtic fields' and thought to date to the Iron Age are likely to be considerably older – from the middle Bronze Age. The pit alignments described earlier which cut off the Biddenham Loop fit well into this picture. Excavations on the edge of the Cambridgeshire Fens have also produced some evidence that ditches may have had accompanying banks topped with a hedge. The field systems in the Ouse Valley would have been to handle large numbers of sheep and/or cattle, and forest clearance would have expanded to accommodate this settled farming pattern.

The science of pollen analysis has allowed archaeologists to map out changes to the prehistoric landscape. Patterns of farming began to change towards the end of the Bronze Age, when the climate became noticeably wetter. Analysis of peat deposits in northern England show the growth of peat after 1200 BC. In the lowlands too, the landscape was changing in response to climate and a growing population. By 1500 BC the lowlands, especially the valleys, were well populated. These land use and social changes were accompanied by a shift to larger tribal groups with an emerging elite. As evidence from more excavations is brought together, this allows a greater understanding of a landscape for the first time. Findings of tree, grass and arable pollen can be used to chart the advance of forest clearance and the change to a countryside dominated by open grassland, then fields.

Counting the grains: pollen analysis and crops in prehistory

Before written records, the history of changes in land use and vegetation can be sketched or roughly mapped out by examining the pollen preserved in deposits such as peat bogs, the mud at the bottom of lakes, and sometimes in soils, if the conditions are favourable. The abundance of pollen produced by many plants, and its robust structure, which combats decay, mean that the detailed examination of a deposit is a worthwhile source of evidence for archaeologists. The technique involves recognising individual pollen grains using a high-powered microscope, then the labour-intensive counting of these grains. Using statistical techniques, it is then possible to estimate the relative distributions of the plants present. Individual tree pollen is relatively easy to separate – for example, lime pollen from oak – but other plants are less accommodating. Up until the extensive land clearing during the later Iron Age, the predominant vegetation was described as 'wildwood', as this best conveys the mosaic of forest types, with lime the most common tree. As these areas were cleared the presence of grass pollen became more frequent, and more herbs (which depend on light reaching the forest floor) are recorded. Plant scientists agree that that elm trees declined markedly at around 3000 BC, but it is uncertain whether this reflects an elm disease or clearance by early farmers. In Bedfordshire, this pollen analysis technique was important in charting the history of peat growth in the Flit Valley. Roman remains at Ruxox Farm, close to Flitwick, show that the peat continued to form after the Roman site was abandoned.

Hill forts and fields: Iron Age farmers in the landscape

In Britain around 800 BC, the technology to smelt iron ore became widespread, mainly due to the ability to generate high temperatures. Iron tools with sharp edges encouraged agricultural expansion and had a significant impact across the landscape. Better tools allowed farming and settlements to expand as land clearance accelerated. Prominent structures such as hill forts now became more common and are one of the archetypal features of the Iron Age in Britain, signalling a growing preoccupation with territory and defence. Examples in Bedfordshire are sited in commanding strategic locations, such as gaps in the Greensand Ridge, or on top of a hill. The exact purpose of these hilltop features is not always agreed upon, but they must have had a defensive role, if only to protect livestock. A very recent study has now brought all the Iron Age forts together in a new atlas, which is available at https://hillforts.arch.ox.ac.uk/. Galley Hill, Sandy Lodge and Caesar's Camp are located on the steep ridges overlooking Sandy and the River Ivel, in the east of the county. There are further good examples, such as Danesborough Camp on the western edge of the ridge, and Craddocks Camp is a possible hill fort overlooking the River Ouzel to the west of Heath and Reach. Mowsbury hill fort on the northern outskirts of Bedford has been dated to the early Iron Age. Excavated in 1971, this site consisted of a single ditch and bank with evidence of a timber fence on top. Mowsbury is a good example of an area that was lived in for a long period of time: in medieval times, the Iron Age ditch was adapted for use as a moat. The landscape was becoming increasingly populated and land was gaining value, making protection and defensive works more important.

The most remarkable settlement evidence comes from the gravel river terraces of the rivers Ouse and Ivel. For the first time in the history of the county, there is unequivocal evidence for the existence of farmers practising a mixed arable/pastoral system. The most dramatic sites are clustered in the Ouse Valley, with the Biddenham Loop, as described in Chapter 1, becoming pivotal to our understanding of the settlement story.

As revealed in *Life in the Loop* and *Close to the Loop* by Albion Archaeology, this area of late Bronze Age/early Iron Age settlement was unenclosed and quite extensive. It contained concentrations of several features, including small pits, and buildings which have left traces of post holes where uprights held the structures in place. Although limited, the evidence suggests that the settlement was permanent and that mixed agriculture was practised. Interestingly, a physical land division, in the form of a pit alignment, was constructed within the Biddenham Loop, suggesting some form of ownership or land management. This has the appearance of a single boundary, designed to 'cut off' the southern two-thirds of the area enclosed by the river's meander. In all, six early/middle Iron Age farmsteads were identified, all sharing similar topographical locations, adjacent to, but above, the river floodplain. Two were close to the earlier settlement, again suggesting some degree of continuity. The key identifying characteristic of each farmstead was the presence of a concentration of large storage pits, which have traditionally been interpreted as seed grain stores. The importance of grains in the diet is shown by the recovery of quern stones used to grind corn. The Higgins Bedford holds a fine example of this type of artefact, unearthed during excavations at Bury Farm, Goldington. Figure 2.1 shows a well-preserved saddle quern, shaped for ease of use (where an upper stone is continually rubbed against a lower stone, with the grain placed between them) which was recovered from this site. This indicates a date in the middle Bronze Age.

Nevertheless, sufficient evidence was found to suggest that mixed farming continued. More excavations in advance of development and road building along the Bedfordshire river terraces have supported this concentration of Iron Age settlements. The extensive gravel workings at the Black Cat roundabout south of Wyboston, where the A1 and A421 meet, has uncovered what seems to be Iron Age field systems with a later Roman occupation on the same site. Settlement seems to have persisted into the period after the Roman withdrawal from Britain, early in the fifth century AD.

Sites continue to be uncovered as housing and infrastructure developments continue, opening up new areas to excavation. Emerging evidence often complements older finds, such as the unearthing of a late Iron Age cemetery at Quince Hill, close to Old Warden. At this site a nineteenth-century antiquary, Thomas Inskip, discovered what has been described as a 'high-class cremation burial', the highlight of which was an urn carved from soft shale rock which is likely to have come from the Portland area of the south coast, where these was a minor industry in the production of elegant pedestal urns and armlets. The Old Warden urn is in the Museum of Archaeology and Anthropology in Cambridge.

Evidence of large-scale settlements and accompanying field systems is now becoming commonplace along the lowland valleys of southern England, including the Bedfordshire rivers. It is clear this was a well settled area, as was the Upper Thames Valley. There is also little doubt that Iron Age settlement was rural, and the population was on the increase towards the end of the period. The sophistication of these farming societies is illustrated by the remarkable and exquisite cast of a cow head found on a site by the River Ouse at Felmersham. This is a casting in bronze, and seems to have been part of a bucket handle.

Figure 2.1a and 2.1b. Quern stones used to grind corn. The base stone and the upper rubbing stone are different types of rock. Image by Vaughan Deane from a collection in The Higgins Bedford.

All of this evidence is hard won by the archaeologist as little, apart from crop marks and occasional pottery which surfaces during ploughing, survives on the surface. The addition of iron tips to ploughs during the Iron Age made cultivation more effective, and pollen from wheat, barley and beans has been found in long-settled areas such as by rivers. Other sites also begin to appear in previously underexploited areas, such as the Greensand Ridge, which has a relatively large number of crop-mark sites all situated on the upper slopes of the ridge. These are undated, but morphological evidence shows that they are probably from the Iron Age to the beginning of Roman settlement. Several ditches and two cremations dating from the Iron Age/Roman period, part of a larger crop-mark complex, were excavated at Sweetbrier Farm west of Old Warden. In a few cases, where limited archaeological investigations of those crop marks have taken place prior to development, both Iron Age and Roman occupation has been confirmed.

Late Iron Age high art
– an enigmatic cow from Felmersham

One of the prized artefacts in The Higgins Bedford is the bronze cast of the head of a cow attached to either end of what is taken to be the handle of a bucket (Figure 2.2). This was excavated from gravel workings in the Great Ouse Valley, close to the village of Felmersham. This is described by archaeologists as a ritual deposit – often a phrase used by professionals when other rational explanations for an object are difficult to find. The discovery was made in 1942 by gravel extractors using a mechanical grab. Other exciting finds included a bronze spout shaped like a fish head, a large bowl, some fragments of pottery and a collection of animal bones. On close inspection, the cow appears to be licking its lips! These artefacts are now one of the highlights of The Higgins Bedford.

By AD 43 this was a settled farming landscape with farms, tracks and perhaps hedged fields, some defended by substantial ditches and banks (such as at Wheathampstead across the Hertfordshire border). Into this countryside came the Roman settlers. This led to a step change in agricultural production to supply a garrison army; the start of commercial wine production; and the beginnings of an organised European trade in agricultural commodities, including perhaps the export of grain from this fertile area of southern England.

Figure 2.2a and b. Felmersham bucket handle. Photograph by Vaughan Dean. Image from a collection in The Higgins Bedford.

CHAPTER 3
BREAD AND WINE:
ROMAN FARMS AND FARMERS (AD 100–400)

'Your corn fields are so productive they assure you of the gifts of Ceres.'
(*Roman court orator*, AD 310)

The conventional picture of the Romans in Britain begins with the construction of Hadrian's Wall in the north of England and reaches its climax with construction of elaborate villas with decorative mosaic floors, such as Fishbourne in Sussex. The Romans as military men, road builders and tax collectors are well established, but as producers of grain and wine, the image is neither so vivid nor so exciting. In the East Midlands landscape, however, it is the Romans' agricultural heritage that is best preserved. There are no elaborate forts, only a few villas, and the military roads, like so many later Roman arterial routes, are simply links to somewhere else. The Romans had a subtle impact on Bedfordshire, and this needs a little unravelling.

In Bedfordshire there are distinct clues to an extensive Roman agricultural presence during the period following the conquest in AD 43 and continuing after the withdrawal of the Roman legions in AD 410. Roman influence continued well beyond this date, and this period is referred to by historians as Romano-British. During and immediately following the Roman withdrawal, widespread grain production was important throughout the east and south of England, with grain being exported from the area to supply military garrisons elsewhere in England and perhaps in Europe. To understand this transition to a stable agricultural economy in the early part of the Roman occupation, it is necessary to consider a number of factors.

First, the weather was improving. Historical accounts show that there was a significant warming in Britain between 250 BC and AD 400. This was known as the 'Roman climatic optimum'. Assessing historical temperatures is never exact, but it is suggested that temperatures were around 1°C degree warmer than today. After AD 400 the weather became less favourable, with increased rainfall making grain production more difficult. The ripening of grapes would have been especially problematic.

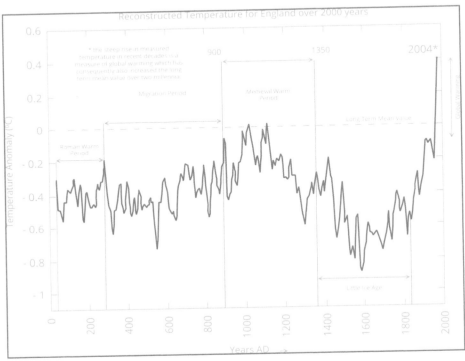

Figure 3.1. This graph shows estimated temperatures in Britain over 2000 years. The most important aspect of this is that distinct periods of higher or lower average temperatures can be identified, which accord with supporting historical evidence. The most discrete spell of higher temperatures coincides with the Roman military presence in Britain, and allowed enhanced grain production and some vine production. (Diagram drawn by John Hambley from data supplied by the author.)

One of the most remarkable features of the Roman period in Europe was the growth of towns. In Britain London, York and Chester (and, more locally, Verulamium, or St Albans) expanded quickly, with a large civilian population living alongside a military garrison. These urban populations depended on a hinterland to supply food, especially wheat for making bread. It is estimated that as many as 50,000 troops were stationed in Britain, adding to a total population of around 3.5 million. This would have strained the ecology, especially given the increased demands for animal fodder. Nevertheless, the importance of Britain was well understood by Roman writers, as the quote at the start of this chapter notes. The full text is:

'Britain, you are indeed blessed… Nature has endowed you with every benefit of land and climate. Your winters are not too cold, nor your summers too hot: your corn fields are so productive they assure you of the gifts of Ceres.'

This speech by a court orator to the Emperor Constantine in AD 310 was given after some 250 years of Roman rule of Britain. However, Britain was still an island, remote and unconnected to the Mediterranean, or Mare Nostrum ('our sea'), as the Romans called it. This required the Roman forces to rely on local food production, rather than food supplied from Europe. Only high-value goods which were worth the transport costs were economic to trade. Agricultural production therefore had to increase markedly to meet the demands of the Roman army and a swelling urban population.

Notes on Figure 3.1

Figure 3.1 was constructed using sources available on the Internet. It is indicative only. Points to be aware of in using this diagram are noted below.

The graph shows the 'temperature anomaly', which is the departure of the temperature from a mean over the 2000-year span. The observation that the majority of the graph is below the baseline of zero degrees reflects the increase in measured temperatures caused by global warming from the mid-nineteenth century onwards. This has raised the average temperature since the beginning of the historic period. In 2015 and 2016 the UK Meteorological Office noted exceptional global temperatures, with both years being above the long-term average from 1961 to 1990. While modern temperatures are derived from actual measurements, the others are estimates from historic records (such as records of good and bad harvests, dates of lambing, extraordinary events recorded such as drought, frost fairs, etc.). Therefore these are only estimates. The correlation with historical periods is recognised by scholars, but the exact dates for the beginning and end of these climatic fluctuations are only approximate.

These agricultural changes were matched by a social transformation. This was a time of opportunity and relative peace. The process of Romanisation was one of education and acculturation, a widening of society so that each tribal unit, which was the backbone of Iron Age society, became a small part of the Roman Empire, and thus the whole world. The Romans made the best use of the available natural resources – especially agriculture and mining. One exceptional advance was the adoption of heavier, iron-shod ploughs, which allowed arable agriculture to move downhill from the thin, shallow soils on the chalk to tackle the more fertile loams in Bedfordshire (and in East Anglia the clay soils on the edges of the fenland). The wooden Roman plough with an iron share (or foot) made a single furrow but did not turn the soil over. Hence, the fields had to be ploughed in both directions, known as 'cross roughing', to create a suitable tilth or seed bed.

In Bedfordshire the soils on the floodplain terraces of the Ouse and Ivel valleys were preferred, just as these areas would be favoured by the market garden industry much later. These soils were fertile loams, workable and flat or gently sloping. Grain from here was exported to Europe, and a clue to the deterioration of climate in the late fourth century AD is the prevalence of grain-drying kilns at Roman sites: wet grain is useless and would rot before transportation. More crop varieties were grown, such as spelt wheat, which replaced the more primitive, low-yielding einkorn types, and this also boosted production. Oats, previously grown but probably not as a cultivated plant, became established, especially in the north of England, where its spread is likely to have been encouraged by the requirements of the Roman cavalry.

The scale of farming also needed to change, and large agricultural estates became common, often with a characteristic field pattern of regular squares. There has been much debate about these regular square fields laid out in a geometric pattern. Traces of this pattern are common in Europe as far north as the Netherlands, but unravelling these relic field patterns in Britain is more difficult. At one time it was thought that this square pattern could be traced in contemporary field patterns around Northill and Broom, but it's very hard to distinguish these from eighteenth-century parliamentary enclosure fields.

The development of Roman settlement can be traced through the remains of country houses founded in the second century AD, which later made way for villa estates. Local examples can be found at Park Street in Hertfordshire, Totternhoe in the south of Bedfordshire, and at Puddlehill close to Houghton Regis. At this latter site, excavators uncovered a number of Roman buildings dated from AD 50–200. The Totternhoe Roman villa, recorded as early as 1904 and excavated during the 1950s, was somewhat later, between AD 250–350. These villa estates would have been agriculturally productive, supplying the growing urban populations at locations such as Dunstable and St Albans. More recent archaeological evidence is revising the picture in this part of England, with Bedfordshire and Northamptonshire being regarded as important agricultural hinterlands and therefore a useful base for tax revenue. Bedfordshire's location – astride Watling Street and Ermine Street, both strategic Roman roads, and also with navigable rivers – gave this area a central importance. Sandy was also an important Roman site, at the intersection of a subsidiary Roman road leading to Godmanchester and Ermine Street, the principal route to York and the north.

The density of Roman settlement within Bedfordshire is still being confirmed, with more sites being discovered as new housing and road developments continue. Such a site is the Romano-British settlement on the River Ouse terraces at the Black Cat roundabout, where the A1 and A421 roads meet. In advance of sand and gravel extraction works, archaeological work has uncovered a late Roman agricultural farming settlement with distinct Iron Age fields continuing in use into the Roman period. There was also a large quantity of Roman pottery and animal bones recovered from the site, suggesting that the farmstead was involved in mixed farming and was in continuous use over a long time. This Romano-British phase of activity was brought to a halt by a large flood that covered the lower-lying areas of the gravel terrace with alluvium, including the site of the Roman farmstead. A later phase in the life of the farmstead shows that people returned to the site after the flood and continued to live there, reopening some of the main ditches and even constructing new buildings. Other finds include a twisted copper alloy bracelet, which suggests that life was prosperous for a farmer in the Roman period. A similar farming settlement at Priory Park in Bedford, also close to the Ouse and located on the gravel terraces, underlines the value of these sites close to the river. The important Roman villa at Radwell in Hertfordshire is another example of Roman occupation and use of a former Iron Age farmstead, giving continuity to the settlement. (The site of the villa is now farmland, but items from the excavation, including a fine marble sculptured head, are held in the University of Cambridge's Museum of Classical Archaeology.)

The only site of Roman occupation in Bedfordshire which could be described as a town would be Dunstable, called Durocobrivae by the Romans. Excavations during the 1960s and 1970s in the town centre uncovered a Roman settlement at the crossroads of Roman Watling Street and the Icknield Way. The settlement was in use for most of the Roman occupation of Britain, certainly from AD 50 to 350. Finds included a Roman cemetery and a water well 28 metres (about 90 feet) deep.

One of the most interesting Romano-British sites is at Ruxox Farm, close to Flitwick, from which a substantial number of artefacts have been recovered, thanks to the diligent work of a local farmer who collected items from the ploughed soil. These finds included small tiles, or tesserae, and the remains of misshapen Venus figurines made from local clay. One of the most intriguing natural discoveries from this site is the growth of peat above the Roman remains, illustrating the increasing wetness of the climate following Roman occupation.

A regional pottery industry known as 'Harrold shelly ware' grew up in north Bedfordshire in the first century AD. Clay subsoil, rich in shell fragments, was extracted from shallow pits in the glacial deposits at Harrold, with a major expansion in production from the early fourth century. The pottery and tile products are found at sites throughout the east and south Midlands. A characteristic of this type of ceramic is a soapy feel to the touch and the visible presence of abundant flakes of shells within the clay.

A change in thinking about Roman history in Bedfordshire took place after recent excavations at a Roman villa at Manton Lane in the suburbs of Bedford. This site, on the edge of the Ouse floodplain, is on a gentle south-facing slope. It was partly excavated between 2012 and 2016. The area has now been re-covered with earth to preserve the structures, pending further archaeological work. These excavations have yielded evidence of a high-status villa, dated to the Roman imperial period (after AD 270). Finds included Harrold ware pottery, a coin, imported glass, and stucco work in plaster that is likely to have been created by continental craftsmen. The villa dates from the high point of Roman colonisation of Britain, and may have been the site of a military office, perhaps acting as a tax-collecting base. The excavators have suggested this site was selected to exercise control over grain being exported east on the River Ouse. The Bedford site is similar to the villa excavated at Bancroft in Milton Keynes, where an extensive coloured mosaic has been uncovered, part of which has been conserved and mounted inside the present-day shopping centre. Like the site at Bedford, Bancroft has been reburied to ensure preservation.

Heavy Romano-British ploughshares have been found as far north as the Scottish Lowlands. These villa estates could have been a place of exile for elite individuals banished from Rome, and later left in the hands of a bailiff after Roman military influence declined. Slave labour or peasant tenants were then recruited to run the villa estates. Elsewhere in Britain, people continued the subsistence style of farming that had been practised since the Iron Age.

The year AD 410 is generally agreed as the end of the Roman occupation of Britain. Climate change is often given as the primary reason for the Romans leaving, and there is no doubt this was a major factor. The best description of this period comes from academic work by Applebaum (1958). He wrote:

'It was not inadequate technique, but inequality of application that was the weak point of Romano-British agriculture. Maladministration, inflation, over-taxation, political insecurity and the consequent social disturbances led to economic disintegration; the increased pressure of the Empire's needs added to a factor beyond human control – climatic deterioration hastened the process of social differentiation and technical decline.'

The breakdown of security therefore meant the end of the villa and, with it, the essential basis of agricultural production. The break-up of the estates had already begun, but in some places the Roman estate farm survived into the Saxon period. However, it was the dispersed peasant holdings perhaps mingled with incoming settlers, who continued to work the fields as a loose community in the vicinity of the ruined residence.

While grain was the primary commodity, the presence of the Roman military, a merchant class, the administrators and a Romanised British population led to a demand for wine. The production of wine in the East Midlands has recently been confirmed at sites along the Nene Valley. Vines were a Roman introduction to Britain, and the fact that they could be grown in southern England marks an improved climate – just as their disappearance from the countryside after AD 400 marks rapidly declining temperatures and increased rainfall. Indeed, the establishment and decline of vineyards is often taken as a proxy for climatic conditions. The return of vineyards to England in the twentieth century is a sign of a return to the climate that was prevalent during the Roman and Romano-British period. Today wine is one of the fastest-growing agricultural sectors in the UK, with an increase in acreage over the past decade of 135 per cent, reflecting warmer summers. The climatic change in temperature is illustrated in Figure 3.1.

Figure 3.2 shows the results of an excavation of a possible Roman vineyard at Ampthill. The site, on a south-facing site overlooking the Flit Valley, was briefly explored prior to a housing development. Excavation in 2010 by the Northamptonshire Archaeological Society examined extensive features left behind by 'Roman plantation agriculture' – possibly a vineyard. The excavation revealed numerous parallel rows laid out for cultivation, probably for growing soft fruit, grapes or hops. What makes this site interesting is its similarity to a site excavated at Wollaston, which also has parallel cultivation rows. The dating evidence from the two sites compare favourably: both are from the late first to early second centuries AD.

The end of the Roman period in Britain is usually fixed as early in the fifth century, when troops were withdrawn. The climate became less attractive, grain had to be dried before storage and shipping, and the vineyards – at least in the north of England and Midlands – were struggling. It is estimated that there was a 10 per cent increase in rainfall beginning in the late fourth century. In the sixth century AD this climatic deterioration continued, due to a number of volcanic eruptions, mainly around the Indonesian islands, from AD 536 to 544, which blocked sunlight.

Roman military investment in Britain was substantial, in terms of manpower and the military infrastructure required by such a force.

At the apex of Roman rule this required a highly productive agricultural chain backed by an efficient supply system, using the well-engineered Roman roads.

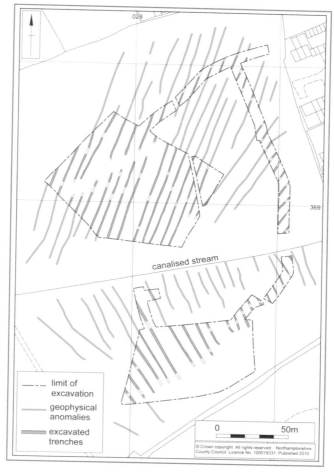

Figure 3.2. A sketch of a possible Roman vineyard at Ampthill. (This figure is reproduced by courtesy of the *Northamptonshire Archaeology Journal.*)

The fragmentation of this integrated social and military machinery did not, however, lead to a retreat from the countryside. Dispersed British farmsteads, with some Roman adoptions, continued to expand well into the sixth century. Increasingly farmers coped with more difficult growing conditions by keeping livestock: the amount of arable land decreased and pollen sequences from Northamptonshire point to a landscape increasingly turned over to grass. These open grasslands prevailed in the fifth and sixth centuries. Into this landscape arrived Saxon – and, later, Scandinavian – farmers with new techniques and social structures. They altered the landscape by creating more concentrated and tightly packed nucleated settlements which today we regard as the normal pattern of the lowland English countryside.

Chateau Nene: Roman vine growing in Bedfordshire and Northamptonshire

The increased security, peace and economic activity in the first two centuries of Roman rule encouraged entrepreneurs to respond to demands for the goods and services required by a substantial garrison and a growing administrative Roman class. Wine was always in demand. It is clear that in pre-Roman Britain the drinking of wine was common – at least, amphorae (or ceramic flasks) used to transport wine from Europe are frequently found on pre-Roman archaeological sites. However, growing vines in Britain became possible with a warming climate, and excavations at Roman villas, houses and military garrisons often turn up grape pips and vine stems. According to historical references, viticulture was already under way in Britain by AD 270. The Romano-British site at Wollaston, Northamptonshire, in the valley of the River Nene, extended to 30 acres and included around 4 miles of trenches, sufficient for an estimated 4000 vines.

In Bedfordshire an intriguing site on the outskirts of Ampthill was excavated in 2009. Here there was a similar pattern of trenches, but no definitive evidence of a vineyard. The scale of this enterprise is impressive: a large area is divided by ditches, with open ground between. Pottery finds are from the second century AD, when the climate would have been optimal for vines. This was clearly a site of Roman plantation agriculture of some type. The Ampthill and Wollaston sites share many common features: the spacing, depth and number of trenches are similar, with the Ampthill site estimated at around 3 miles of trenches, adequate for over 3000 vines. There is evidence from surface markings on the pottery found in the trenches that manure or compost, or both, was added to the vines. Archaeologists concluded that the type of crop grown at Ampthill cannot be confirmed, but viticulture is one of the most plausible explanations. It is reasonable to conclude that senior Roman officers and officials drank imported vintages, while the mercenaries on Hadrian's Wall made do with Chateau Nene. Honey would have been added to local wine to make it more palatable.

CHAPTER 4
NEW ARRIVALS – MIGRANTS, SETTLERS AND TRADERS (410–1066)

The Saxons: farmers and villagers

The shift in climatic conditions which accelerated the departure of the Roman armies was clearly not confined to Britain. Settlers who had earlier expanded into the more marginal lands of north-west Europe also needed to reassess the options for farming in a less favourable climate. Archaeological evidence shows this as a time of rising sea levels, flooding many low-lying settlements along the large European rivers and forcing farmers to build artificial islands and move to higher land. The period from the fifth to the eighth century AD has been labelled by European historians as the migration period – or the 'Volkerwanderung' ('people movement' in German), a term mostly applied to the movement of central European tribes. The climate likely reached a low point around AD 500, but this period was further disrupted by severe famines in AD 535 and 536, most likely caused by the volcanic eruptions (mentioned at the end of Chapter 3) in the tropics, which impacted the amount of sunlight in the northern hemisphere.

Whatever the causes, the result was a significant movement of tribes and peoples across Europe, filling the vacuum left by the departure of the Roman armies. The emergence of mobile continental tribes became, after a few generations, an outward migration of Saxon farmers westward from the north German plain and across the North Sea. They arrived along the coast of eastern England in several waves, and met little opposition. The Roman forts which had offered a line of defence had long been abandoned. The arriving settlers made use of the major rivers to travel inland, including the Thames, and the rivers that flow into the Wash offered easy access from the sea into the heartland of England. By AD 500 there is evidence of Germanic people along the rivers Welland, Great Ouse, Nene and Cam. By around AD 550, the Anglo-Saxon kingdoms of Northumbria, Mercia, Wessex, Kent and East Anglia had taken on their historic form and had begun to expand. In addition to using the waterways, people used elevated routes such as the chalk downs, including the Icknield Way, to reach further into Britain.

However, these Anglo-Saxons immigrants did not arrive and settle an abandoned landscape on which they imposed new types of settlement and farming. By the time of the Roman military departure, the English rural landscape had largely been cleared and settled into dispersed farms and hamlets, each surrounded by its own fields, and this pattern of countryside persisted into the sixth century. The new arrivals were quick to take advantage of new opportunities and transfer techniques and farming experience from Europe – techniques such as improved ploughs and, most importantly, a transformation of the farming and social systems by the move to open field farming with three or four large shared fields. These ideas were all nurtured in Europe and quickly spread across lowland England.

Older interpretations of history described the Saxon period as a time of turmoil and bloodshed – the invasion of Germanic hordes. However, there is now a reinterpretation of this view, seeing history as continuity – the Roman-British working the land in isolated farmsteads, with a connecting line back to the Iron Age. The Saxons, once described by Roman chroniclers as the fiercest of the tribes in Europe, converted to Christian farmers, traders and finally artisans, grouped in a collection of kingdoms from Northumberland to Wessex. The tribes described in the Roman chronicles as 'warriors eager for fame' became settled farmers and livestock keepers. Eventually the rural economy began to adapt and cope with the significant changes brought about by the departure of the Roman garrisons. There was less demand for grain to feed the military, and less tax to pay. Arable land was turned over to pasture and the economy moved to local exchange (or barter) without using coins.

In Bedfordshire, settlement can be mapped by the distribution of Saxon place names, especially along the Great Ouse Valley. Settlement names ending in '-ham' indicate a Saxon farm or homestead – Biddenham, Bromham and Pavenham are examples from Bedfordshire. One such place name is Odell, now thought to refer to the cultivation of woad, an important and valued crop well into the medieval period (Woad Hill then became Odell in modern usage). Other words in rural use have survived, such as 'hedge', which has echoes in the Dutch word 'heg' and German 'heche', and can be traced back to the Saxon livestock keepers who needed to control animals by a living boundary, not merely a temporary fence.

Prior to the Saxon farming revolution, the field pattern within Bedfordshire still owed much to Iron Age (or earlier) settlers, and some surviving relic rectangular Roman fields. This radical change began the process of a social change from farmstead and hamlets which were dispersed to what we now know as the English village. However, by the time the Domesday commissioners began to meticulously record the holdings in every corner of England after 1086, it was a very different landscape, with new villages surrounded by extensive open ploughed fields. This transformation has been described as the 'Mid-Saxon Shuffle', and took place around the eighth and ninth centuries when people found village life more appealing than living on more isolated farmsteads. The open field system also required co-operation and a communal approach to the management of land, so villages or clustered settlements became the norm.

This was not only a technological transformation but a social change that locked a community into a farming calendar. Individuals became small cogs in the machine of village farming. This massively boosted production, making it attractive to local landlords, and open field, community-managed agriculture expanded across the country. The social organisation required was impressive. A significant expanse of arable land was required, and the owner had to have the authority to impose the change from individual to communal farming. The land was partitioned into three or sometimes four great fields, and then further subdivided into furlongs, then into strips named selions. Meadow land was also shared, and where the land became more marginal, and therefore less useful for growing arable crops, 'common' or 'waste' land was available to all for open grazing. The social complications of this farming method should not be underestimated: they involved the entire farming community acknowledging a set of regulations, and obligations, backed by sanctions.

Many Bedfordshire villages, such as Turvey, with its Saxon church of St Peter's, date from this period. By the year 1000, almost all present-day English villages were established, many with a name that can be traced to their Saxon or Viking origin.

Prior to the removal of hedges in the 1970s to maximise the land that could be planted, and to allow larger tractors and equipment to be used efficiently, the arable open field system could still be seen across middle England. Bedfordshire is a county of clay soils, often intractable and wet in the spring, which have been transformed by field drainage to become arable land. Nevertheless, the pattern of relic ridge and furrow in grass fields around Potsgrove and Stanbridge, with scattered examples in north Bedfordshire, is still clear (Figure 4.1).

Figure 4.1. Relic ridge and furrow ploughing. This LiDAR image makes visible the relic ploughing in pasture at Little Staughton, north Bedfordshire. The image is derived from a dataset of radar imagery placed in the public domain by the Environment Agency. © Environment Agency, 2015. All rights reserved.

The presence of these ancient agricultural landscapes can now be recognised by radar devices mounted on aircraft. Sensitive instruments are capable of measuring small changes in the land surface level, such as ridge and furrow undulations. Recent systematic flying by the Environment Agency has provided archaeologists with a new library of airborne images, many of which show good examples of medieval ploughing, including some from north Bedfordshire. At Laxton in Northamptonshire, this open field farming system is still practised today: farmers work collectively on shared land, with decisions made each year by on crops and management. The relic pattern of ridge and furrow still persists on land that has been grassed over since the contraction of farming in the later medieval period. A long-serving cricket umpire once told me that several Bedfordshire cricket outfields still have these undulations. In a neat conjunction of historical evidence, the field at Manton Lane, Bedford, excavated in 2015–16 to reveal a late Roman villa, was the last remaining ridge and furrow field within the town boundary.

The Saxon settlers used a fixed, non-reversible plough pulled by an unwieldy team of six, perhaps eight, oxen. As the plough team advanced, the soil or sods were thrown to the right. Turning the plough team at the end of the furrow was a challenge, and the ploughman tended to anticipate this by bending the furrow slightly at the end, giving a slight 'S' shape to the strip. On returning in the opposite direction the sods were again to the right, forming a ridge. In contrast, a modern plough can simply be reversed by the flick of a switch. The ploughing of arable fields required well-managed, well-fed oxen teams, and advances in the technology of ploughing were beginning to affect how the land was managed. A considerable area of pasture was required to feed livestock: this underlined the importance of fallow fields and commons in the emerging three-field system, which was ended by enclosure in the eighteenth century.

Being close to a river, which offered a means of transport, was important to these farmers, and a sizeable Saxon cemetery containing pots and urns, excavated in the 1980s, is evidence of a substantial Saxon town where Kempston now stands. The site, now a Sainsbury's supermarket, yielded some fabric, brooches and belts, and an extraordinary glass beaker which is now held in the British Museum alongside wonderful artefacts from sites such as the Sutton Hoo ship burial.

Bedfordshire became a county of village farming, with its diverse resources used to sustain a variety of livelihoods. The Saxons were assiduous users of wood, and forest clearance proceeded apace. At the same time, they recognised the value of woodland and managed woodland grazing by pigs (known as pannage). By the year 1000, Cranfield was reported as having a thousand pigs. The importance of wood resource is reflected in the range of uses to which wood was put: wooden plates and bowls, bedding for livestock in winter, fuel for the blacksmith, wood coppicing produced poles for building, and when times were bad the woods became the larder of last resort. Livestock keepers were only allowed to release their swine late in the year to avoid them destroying new growth in the forest – so important for a long-term sustainable woodland. Saxon land use was on a continuum from the village outward across the ploughed land to pasture, to managed woodland, and finally the wild woods or forests. These woods and forests were important for hunting – still a democratic pursuit prior to the Norman imposition of draconian restrictions on who could benefit from wild game.

Tracks such as the Icknield Way continued to be used, and there is evidence for a footway – the Thede Way – crossing Bedfordshire around Chalgrave and Leighton Buzzard. The pattern of township boundaries provides some evidence that this ancient route is perhaps the earliest identifiable topographical feature in the area. It was certainly a Saxon route on the line of an earlier, perhaps originally prehistoric path, connecting the Icknield Way north of Luton to Wing in Buckinghamshire. This included a five-mile stretch through the Leighton Buzzard district, crossing the River Ouzel at Yttingaford (now Tiddenfoot), the scene of the signing of a peace treaty with the Danes in AD 906. The Thede Way was obviously significant in the landscape and used in boundary definition at that time.

The most informative record of the period comes from the *Anglo-Saxon Chronicle*, which is the single most important source for the history of early England, filling the gap left by the Romans and before the arrival of the Normans. This is where we first read of the much later arrival of Danes – the Vikings of Scandinavia. At this point Bedford and the Great Ouse Valley became a frontier, with Saxon settlement to the north and west, and the Danes receiving tribute (in the form of Danegeld payments) to the east. Offa, building his English empire on the coat-tails of Europe, settled the Great Ouse Valley. It is reasonable to assume that Bedfordshire was relatively prosperous at this time, with a wool industry that contributed to the export trade from the east coast ports. Certainly early attempts at civil administration had begun, with the first mention of 'shires', including Bedfordshire. However, strife was common and there are recorded battles – or at least skirmishes – with the Danish forces who arrived at Bedford and in the Lea Valley, by AD 914.

Danes and Vikings – raiders, traders and settlers

The exact reason for the movement of people from Scandinavia to Britain in the ninth century is still not fully understood by scholars, but it is realistic to conclude that this was one strand of the migration period which influenced the earlier Germanic Saxon tribes. There were both push and pull factors involved: archaeologists have noted the increase in grave sites in Scandinavia and Iceland at this period, suggesting that the available land was under pressure. Since the amount of land suitable for farming and food production was always very limited, the impulse to strike outward was therefore strong. In eastern England, Viking raids were common and traumatic.

The invasion of northern Scandinavian invaders and settlers (who we know collectively as the Vikings) happened at the same time as the movement of people from North Germany and the area that is now Denmark. The people who came to this area of England are known as 'the Danes' – hence Danish Camp, to the east of Bedford.

The climate was clearly a factor. By AD 950 the steady improvement in summer temperatures can be seen in tree ring growth, and what scholars now refer to as the Medieval Warm Period (MWP), or the Medieval Climate Anomaly, was under way. Long sea voyages became less hazardous. Iceland, Greenland and even North America were now feasible and attainable destinations.

In Bedfordshire, as elsewhere along the south and east coast, the Viking raiders were from the Jutland area of Denmark, hence the historical description of these invaders as 'the Danes'. However, this is not always accurate – the site on the River Ouse now known as Danish Camp is likely not to have much direct Viking history at all.[2] What we do know is that these raiders crossing the North Sea used the navigable rivers such as the Great Ouse and attacked Bedford. A Viking burial at Harrold dated to the ninth century contained practical items, such as a whetstone and fragments of what might have been an iron bucket: by AD 875 Bedford was a Danish town, not retaken by the Saxon kingdom of Mercia until AD 915.

---

[2] The Historic Environment Record entry does not directly refer to the Danish camp. The earliest record referring to this site dates from the eleventh century, a hundred years or so after the Battle of Bedford, when the site became a moated homestead.

Again the *Anglo-Saxon Chronicle* provides a concise picture:

'At the same time the [Danish] army came from Huntingdon and East Anglia and made the fortress at Tempsford, and took up quarters in it and built it, and abandoned the other fortress at Huntingdon, thinking that from Tempsford they would reach more of the land with strife and hostility. And they went till they reached Bedford; and the men who were inside went out against them, and fought against them and put them to flight, and killed a good part of them.'

It is clear that Bedfordshire became a frontier, a disputed land on the margins of what became the Danelaw. The relationship between the Saxons and the Danes was eventually settled, leading to a recognised boundary that defined their territories. This boundary line could be traced up the Thames from the sea, then followed the course of the Lea northwards to its source at Leagrave, striking due north to Bedford and westwards along the Great Ouse as far as the Roman road at Watling Street. Beyond this, its limits are less well defined.

During the early tenth century Bedford prospered as a town, and with this came a growth in power of landowners – land began to be centralised into manors. At Raunds in Northamptonshire, older scattered settlements were replaced by a larger village and a planned landscape when the area moved from Danish to Saxon control. This was becoming the new agricultural landscape. It was already prevalent in north-west Europe, and later became formalised into a rigid social order when Norman control imposed a feudal hierarchy.

Land was becoming more valuable: at Chalgrave, close to Toddington, a charter from AD 926 records a land transaction between the landlord and a tenant who was granted five hides of land (600 acres). The boundaries were set out in a legal agreement. An interesting point is the incorporation of an earlier Roman road to mark one boundary. This shows that land was now of significant value: it was necessary to have a legal document to define the asset and record its limits.

Into this settled landscape arrived the Norman military machine with knights and castles, moated settlements, and land reserved for the hunt. Land was transferred to a Norman elite, seemingly without great unrest, and a social order established based on an estate with a manor at the centre surrounded by a pattern of large open fields worked by labourers. The previous, more egalitarian social order was replaced by changes in land ownership, and the feudal estate became the prevalent farming model. This period of social engineering began with making a record of who owned what, and how valuable these assets were – the Domesday Book. Land was now a recognisable asset and ownership was legalised, protected, and given a monetary value.

Measuring the land: hides, virgates and acres

Medieval documents are often concerned with land: who owns it, what it is used for, what is worth, and – importantly – whether it can be taxed. The Domesday Book records woodland and gives this a value in terms of how many pigs the area can support. At Aspley Guise in Bedfordshire, for example, fifty pigs were recorded. This number would inform the mediaeval bureaucracy of the approximate size of the woodland and the quality of the grazing. However, translating this type of information into modern land measurement units is a challenge, as the record is framed by the use to which the land is put, rather than its dimensions. Historians have called this a 'fiscal acre', to emphasis its value for a specific use, rather than its size.

The Saxon unit land unit was known as a 'hide'. This was then subdivided into four areas known as 'virgates', each of which was approximately 30 acres. This was the area of land that could be ploughed by a team of two oxen in one season. However, this varied across the landscape and is also a measure of use or value, rather than size. A hide is then approximately 120 acres (50 hectares), which was widely understood to be enough land to support a family. This needs to be qualified for a modern audience: a 'family' could be a kin group of variable size rather than a modern nuclear family.

The term 'hide' was used in AD 990 to raise a tax to pay to the Danish invaders, and was later used as the basic unit of value in the Domesday Book, in which Bedfordshire arable land totalled 1200 hides, and Northamptonshire just less than twice this figure. The geld (or tax) levied in 1193–94 was based on a rate per hide.

CHAPTER 5
THE CAMPAIGN FOR INFORMATION –
THE NORMANS AND THE DOMESDAY BOOK
(1086–CIRCA 1300)

'Then he sent his men all over England into every shire and had them find out how many hundred hides there were in the shire, or what land and cattle the king himself had in the country, or what dues he ought to have in twelve months from the shire.'

(*The Anglo-Saxon Chronicle*)

The arrival of the Normans in 1066 heralded the construction of the great buildings which are now so familiar to us, and which provide a backdrop to so much English history. The Normans built ramparted castles or fine cathedrals in many British cities. Even in rural England the simple mottes (Figure 5.1), with or without a bailey, are reminders of the Normans' dominant military presence. Capped with wooden towers, these early Norman mounds would have been an imposing sight in the countryside. Some of the more highly fortified motte and bailey castles were superimposed upon existing villages or town settlements, such as the castle mound in Bedford, by the River Great Ouse, which is still a prominent feature. There are Norman castles at strategic points along the Greensand Ridge, such as Cainhoe Castle close to the River Flit and other mottes on top of the northern Greensand scarp slope, such as at Exeter Wood. Away from this high land there are prominent mottes visible at Flitwick, Yieldon and Pirton. Totternhoe Castle is the largest motte and bailey castle in Bedfordshire: its importance is shown by the commanding position it holds on the chalk downs overlooking the valley of the River Ouzel. Dressed stone at the site indicates the presence of a masonry building, evidence for which may well survive below the present ground surface. The land was granted to Dunstable Priory for a quarry operation in the twelfth century, which became a substantial source of income for the priory.

Figures 5.1a and b. Cainhoe motte, Clophill. Figure 5.1a is a modern photograph of the site, taken by the author. Figure 5.1b is a painting of the Norman motte and bailey earthwork by Edward Callam, an Elstow-based artist who painted many rural scenes in Bedfordshire in the 1950s. (This painting is included in the UK Art Collection, and is held by Luton Culture in the collection at Wardown Museum. Reproduced here with permission.)

Later, towards the close of the thirteenth century, rural life became unsettled and defensive site were increasingly valued. Bedfordshire is especially rich in moated sites, with one of the densest concentrations in England, estimated at around 300. An example is the recently excavated site at Sharnbrook Close, now within a local nature reserve. Here the excavators recorded a mid-twelfth-century domestic moated site within a distinctive ringwork. Outside the defensive area there is evidence of crude flooring paved with river-worn cobbles from the Ouse to create a dry standing, most likely for horses or other livestock. Moats such as this are often associated with patterns of dispersed settlement and irregular field systems. The origin of many such moats is associated with 'assarting' – the creation of new farmland out of woodland. This was common in the twelfth and thirteenth centuries as the population grew and the countryside prospered. The main concentration of moats is in the north of Bedfordshire, as farmers began to expand the land they cultivated and moved to farm the more intractable clay soils that are common north of the Ouse Valley.

The Norman preoccupation with organisation and documentation reached a peak in the comprehensive recording of land in the Domesday Book. This survey was held in awe by people at the time, and was known as the King's Book. The Great Domesday Book[3] provides a unique insight into land distribution in the thirty-one counties of England between the Channel and the River Tees. Completed astonishingly rapidly during 1086 and 1087, the Domesday Book is the first public record of land, providing tax information on Saxon England for the Norman bureaucracy, for military and civilian administration. This was a campaign for information. The Domesday Book could be described as the original land database for England: the next attempt on such a scale was not made until 1873. Defence, and the 'geld' or tax required to fund the building of mottes and castles, was the principal motivation for undertaking this mammoth task. In France in 1066, barons, bishops and even monasteries

---

3 There is also a Little Domesday Book covering East Anglia (Essex, Norfolk and Suffolk). This information was never added to the larger Great Domesday Book.

The Campaign for Information

were duty-bound to provide their quote of military personnel to the Duke of Normandy. This arrangement was simply transferred to England.

The Norman bureaucracy, and especially the king, required an understanding of, and information on, alternative power sources in the realm – the major landowners and the church. This could then be used to fine, seize land or to demand military support – it became an effective instrument of control.

The character of the king is important in understanding the reasoning behind such a monumental record. William has been described as a ruthless pragmatist with a degree of avarice, who insisted on efficient administration. His goal was to bind all his subjects into a feudal system in which the laws were clear – and obeyed. As Simon Schama (2000) explains: *'it was as if William had conquered the kingdom all over again, this time statistically and in a form that no disgruntled motte and bailey baron would ever overcome.'*

The king was not interested in recording history; he wanted to 'make a survey of all … the devices and payments due from each and every estate'. Therefore the Domesday Book was a record of the estates of England. The names within the text are the names of estates, not always villages. Some estates may have contained no villages at all while others had only a scatter of farmsteads and hamlets. So the appearance of a village name in the Domesday Book is not necessarily proof that it existed in 1086.

This enthusiasm for organisation and order introduced a new term to English: the word 'manor' occurs often in the survey, and this became the word used to describe the land held both within the demesne of the lord and land rented to tenants. This Norman idea builds on the late Saxon trend of consolidating land, and the arrival of Norman governance simply accelerated this process begun by the Saxons. The characteristics of a manor came to be recognised as a consolidated estate where the lord controlled the land and had the right to demand labour from the occupants. Serfdom became a Norman institution.

Bedfordshire is recorded in folio 209 of the Domesday Book. The record is ordered in a strict hierarchical way, with each entry following a consistent pattern. It begins with the land owned by the king, such as at Leighton Buzzard, Luton and Houghton Regis, then continues with the land owned by bishops, beginning with the Bishop of Bayeux. The list of ecclesiastical landowners is lengthy. Following Bayeux, land was held by Bishop Coutances in France, Lincoln and Durham, and then the ownership of individual churches was listed, such as St Paul's Cathedral in London. Eventually, there is land held by individuals, such as the Countess Judith at Maulden, and by groups, such as the Burgesses of Bedford. Individual records provide an insight into the distribution of land in Bedfordshire. At Old Warden in 1086, for example, we meet Azelina, the wife of Ralph Tallboys, who held half a hide (around 60 acres). Her tenant was Walter the Monk. The unravelling of these land area measures can be confusing – they are summarised in the box below.

The Domesday Book – the first land database

Each Domesday record follows the same sequence. First, the area of land is listed using a measure known as a 'hide', which is assumed to be around 120 acres and should be capable of maintaining a family. The hide was the basic unit of tax assessment (or geld). Next came the number of plough teams required to work the arable land, followed by the economically active population (such as peasants, cottagers, and finally slaves). Interesting additional information is then listed – such as the presence of a mill, areas of meadow or woodland for pigs – and last the overall land value is noted.

An example is Cotton End on the outskirts of Bedford, held by Nigel d'Aubigny and assessed as just over three hides, with land for six plough teams. Five 'villains' (peasants) work this land in addition to eleven cottagers, who were of a lower status. Woodland for 100 pigs is recorded, and the overall value of the land is 60 shillings. Nigel d'Aubigny crops up again in Maulden, with an interesting reference to 25 acres, which is recorded as being 'taken in unjust possession to the loss of the men who held the land'.

This record for Old Warden also illustrates a common feature in the Domesday Book, which is a fall in land values following the Norman invasion. Azelina's modest piece of land was valued by the commissioners at 10 shillings, whereas the land was previously held by the splendidly named Eric the Bald, and valued at 20 shillings. The decline is best explained by the Norman military machine destroying land, crops and buildings, and ruining the countryside as the armies crossed Bedfordshire on their way to quell revolts in northern England. (This response to revolts, in the winter of 1069–70, was brutal and is now referred to as the 'harrying of the North' by historians.)

The other significant feature of the Norman preoccupation with land management is the requirement to set aside areas in which to hunt. This meant that the law became stricter in defining Royal Forests as exclusive hunting reserves; local people no longer had access to this land, which was previously valuable for fuel and game. The modern meaning of *'forest'* is an area of wooded land. However, in the Middle Ages it meant closer to the modern idea of a closed reserve, which was land legally set aside for royal hunting. In 1217 the laws were eased by a Charter of the Forest, which restored some public rights of access to Royal Forests. In recognising these rights, this charter complemented the Magna Carta and was arguably more significant for the rural population.

In November 2017, the Woodland Trust launched a Charter for Trees, Woods and People to mark the 800 years since this landmark agreement which allowed the common people to once again use woodlands as a means of supplementing their livelihood. However, in many areas the older laws still prevailed and were strictly enforced, even after the 1217 Charter.

New Norman laws superseded the prior Anglo-Saxon system in which rights to the forest included not only woods, but also heath, moorland and wetlands. These areas were not exclusive to the king or nobles, but were shared among the people. In contrast, the new Norman forest laws were harsh, forbidding not only the hunting of game in the forest, but also the cutting of wood and the collection of fallen timber, berries, or anything growing in the forest. The law was designed to protect the *venison* and the *vert*, the noble animals of the chase – deer and wild boar – and the greenery that sustained them. At the height of this exclusion in the late twelfth and early thirteenth centuries, fully a third of the land of southern England was designated as Royal Forest; at one stage in the twelfth century, all of Essex was afforested, and on his accession Henry II declared all of nearby Huntingdonshire a Royal Forest. In Bedfordshire there is no record of such royal enclosures, presumably since there was much good hunting land elsewhere. However, local landowners were quick to follow this trend, which continued up to and beyond the time of Henry VIII, who took delight in the hunting opportunities at Ampthill, for example.

The open field with two communally worked fields was the beginning of what is sometimes called a 'champion landscape' – from the French 'champaigne', meaning a farmed countryside. While this was the most efficient way to exploit arable land and the labour force, this system of farming required large teams of oxen for ploughing, and the oxen required one field large enough to supply animal fodder. The need for communal tools and shared labour also became critical. The changing pattern was a factor in moving the operation of an estate on to a feudal arrangement with organised farming and labour available in a central village.

The weak points in such a farming system were the requirement to maintain the soil's fertility, hence the importance of manure, and the limited area of meadow and grazing required to support the hungry oxen. In the Domesday Book, there are 8000 records for plough teams, with about a quarter of the land being ploughed for planting grain in any one year. Both these points were to become central in the arguments to move to individual enclosed holdings in the seventeenth century, and this reached a climax with the parliamentary enclosures of the eighteenth and nineteenth centuries. The improvement in the design of ploughs was also important: during the late Saxon period the common Roman plough (or ard), which did little more than scratch the surface of the soil, and required cross-ploughing to achieve a suitable seed bed, was replaced by a mould-board plough that was capable of turning the soil over. This buried weeds and brought nutrients to the surface, but required stronger, well-fed oxen.

As outlined earlier, the open field farming system emerged in the Saxon period and mirrored the landholdings already established in Europe. It proved to be an efficient system for landowners to manage their extensive estates, as recorded in the Domesday Book. The model then expanded to three fields, as new areas were cleared and established to meet the challenge of feeding a growing population. Previous chapters have mentioned the importance of Bedfordshire as a granary, and this is underlined by the number of mills noted in the Domesday Book – around 100 in the county.

Norman expansion was aided by a relatively favourable climate which encouraged the settlement of marginal and more remote land, especially on the Greensand Ridge. A number of monastic sites were established, including the Cistercian abbeys at Woburn and Old Warden and the Gilbertine Priory at Chicksands. Only a few of the former monastic sites on the Greensand Ridge have been extensively studied or investigated archaeologically.

One site which has been studied is at Old Warden in central Bedfordshire, founded in 1135 by the local lord, Walter Espec. The Cistercians were especially keen to gain God's approval by clearing what they liked to describe as desolate land or 'waste' on the margins of existing settlements. The motive, outwardly at least, was to seek solitude and pray. This important abbey survived for 400 years until the dissolution of the monasteries initiated by Henry VIII in 1537. Old Warden was the first of the larger monasteries to be closed.

One feature of this substantial and important abbey was a vineyard, which provides evidence for the return of a benign climate. The abbey was at its peak in the twelfth and thirteenth centuries and it is estimated that during this period vines were grown on nearly 30 per cent of the abbey precinct. Remarkably, a part of the Little Vineyard was replanted in 1986 and today this site is again producing grapes – and award-winning white wines. Listed in monastic records is also a hopground. However, this would have been a relatively late feature in the abbey's history as hops did not arrive in England until the early sixteenth century. At Chicksands, the estate map of 1855 clearly has a field called the Hopgrounds, and an adjacent building including a hop store. This field name makes it through to the 1883 Ordnance Survey map. This area is now within the Sandy Smith Nature Reserve, near Clophill.

The clearing of woods to cultivate more land was a feature of Cistercian agriculture. This eventually led to an abbey running monastic farms, or granges, worked by lay brothers, alongside other properties worked by tenants. The extensive properties managed from Old Warden Abbey are illustrated in Figure 5.2: there were sixteen within modern Bedfordshire and several in neighbouring counties. The grain mills operated by the abbey are also marked. The table on page 49 lists other important religious houses in Bedfordshire.

The monastic grange:
Cistercian farms and farmers

The grange or monastic farming system was central to the economic viability of Cistercian settlements throughout rural Europe, and became the model in England. The purpose of a grange was to contribute to the sustainability of the monastic community it served, while at the same time being self-sufficient. These farms operated largely outside the manorial system, allowing the monks to manage their business interests without being restricted by feudal rules. This placed them at a significant advantage over other landholders, which did not always make the brothers popular. Additionally, they were able to take a long-term view on the planning and development of their estates, with the result that patterns of land use evolved over time in response to broader social and economic trends.

By the end of the fifteenth century, all the granges had been leased to tenants with a few exceptions (such as farms close to the abbey at Rowney and the neighbouring Park grange). There are a number of reasons for moving to tenanted farms – most likely a lack of labour in rural areas following the numerous outbreaks of plague, disease and famine. These stopped being granges in the original sense.

In theory, the Cistercian Order spaced granges across the landscape. Granges were required to be no more than a day's walk from the monastery to which they belonged – which could be anything up to 20 miles. Furthermore, there should be least 5 miles between granges belonging to different Cistercian houses. Fountains Abbey in northern England boasted twenty-six granges – more than any other abbey in Britain, although Old Warden came a close second with twenty-three. The largest grange within the reach of Old Warden was Park, which worked 663 acres, of which 180 acres were arable land and 180 acres pasture. In addition the holding at Park included smaller areas of meadow and a rabbit warren.

'For the Good of the people and the saving of my Soul': The religious houses in Bedfordshire.

LOCATION	ORDER	FOUNDED	MOTHER HOUSE	NOTES
Elstow	Benedictine nunnery	About 1078		Founded by William the Conqueror's niece, Judith
Warden	Cistercian	1135	Rievaulx, Yorkshire	
Woburn	Cistercian	1145	Fountains Abbey, Yorkshire	
Dunstable	Augustine	1132		One of the largest in Bedfordshire
Newnham	Augustinian	1166		
Caldwell	Augustine			
Chicksands	Gilbertine	About 1150		On the Greensand Ridge
Bushmead	Augustine	About 1195		
Harrold	Augustinian nuns	About 1138		

Mills and Granges of Warden Abbey

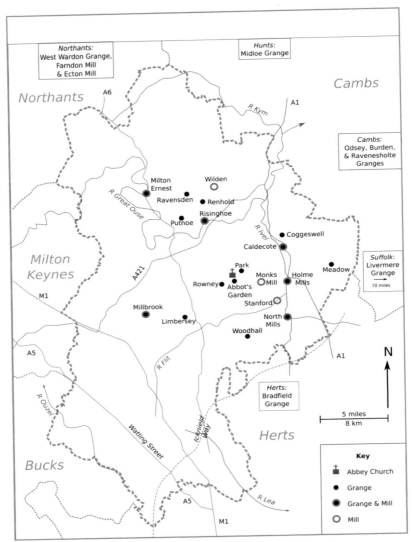

Figure 5.2. Sites of granges and mills operated by Warden Abbey. (Information from Margaret Roberts and map by Ian Baillie.)

Fish formed an important part of the diet of the community at Warden. The remains of fish breeding ponds are still visible, as is the feeder tank or dam used to control the water flow to the abbey. The importance of fish in the diet of both the common people and in the monastic communities is illustrated by the mention of the deregulation of fish weirs in the Magna Carta of 1215. Clause 33 requires the removal of these weirs, which were designed to harvest fish for the benefit of a few and prevent the less well-off from gaining access to fish. The clause required that 'all fish weirs shall be removed from the Thames and the Medway and throughout the whole of England'.

This harvesting of fish required traps and baskets woven from osiers, or willow branches. At Flitton Moor there is a patch of willow planted for this purpose and formerly managed to yield the most useful thickness of willow lengths. Harvesting of osiers from the moor is noted in thirteenth-century historical records from Flitton parish.

The consolidation of land by the monasteries followed the model of the larger estates, and landholdings of 400 acres became common. The produce of these estates was processed at grain mills along the rivers of Bedfordshire and beyond. However, 'fulling mills', which processed wool from the sheep flocks the Cistercian brothers were so keen on, also became a feature. This is important in the Bedfordshire context as, much later, Fuller's earth, which is the essential ingredient is cleaning the oil from fleece, was extracted from quarries at Clophill and Aspley. However, there are no records of the use of these specialist clays at this time.

Figure 5.3. The Warden Abbey water supply header tank. This small reservoir or header tank is still visible adjacent to the Warden Abbey site on the Greensand Ridge. (Image by the author.)

A dominant landlord in central Bedfordshire at this time was Nigel d'Aubigny, who was very much a part of the Norman nobility. His influence lives on in the visible remains of the motte close to the village of Clophill. He appointed a steward to administer his lands at Ampthill, which became Ampthill Great Park, and later his son Henry gave land for a religious settlement at Beadlow, encouraged no doubt by his family connections to St Albans Abbey Church. At this time, many landowners also held land in France, and were especially keen to foster religious connections with the monastic mother houses across the channel.

The French Connection:

Nigel d'Aubigny in Bedfordshire

After the king and the Bishop of Bayeux, the Bishop of Coutances was the third most important landowner in Bedfordshire, as recorded in the Domesday Book. The bishop held land at Melchbourne (assessed as ten hides, worth £8). It is thought that Nigel d'Aubigny (sometimes referred to as Nigel d'Albini), who became a significant landowner in Bedfordshire, was also from the Bayeux region of Normandy. D'Aubigny made his headquarters at Cainhoe in the Flit valley to the east of Clophill and built a substantial Norman motte there with two extensive baileys. The obligation to the king from this estate was military service by twenty-five knights, and his landholdings were granted to followers such as Nigel de Wast, who held Ampthill and Millbrook. Silsoe was granted to his mistress (noted as: 'In Silsoe a certain concubine of Nigel holds two hides'). D'Aubigny has a section to himself in the Domesday Book, listing lands held at Husborne Crawley, Tingrith, Harlington and twenty-seven other estates. Later Robert d'Aubigny funded a small monastery at Beadlow in about 1140, which provided priests for Cainhoe and Clophill until 1428, when it had become too small to be sustainable. Today there is no visible evidence of its existence.

The next level of landowning elite were those not rich or influential enough to build a castle or fund a monastic settlement, but who were ready to advertise their increasing wealth and status by digging a moat, which could be flooded. Why did moats become such a feature of the countryside in the thirteenth century, when there seemed to be no security threats that would require defensive and expensive earth-moving? Over 300 moated sites have been identified in Bedfordshire, often in wet and tenacious clays. The excavation of a moat would require significant labour – and funds. The persistence of these sites is often reflected in common place names such as Moat Farm.

By the end of the thirteenth century, the rise in countryside poverty and insecurity, including gangs, may have gone some way to explaining these moated sites. The lack of manpower in rural England saw an end to this form of settlement after the plague from 1350 onwards. Moats may have been used as fish farms, but there seems to be a consensus that they were to display wealth, with the bonus of providing additional security. A parallel could perhaps be made with a gated community in a peaceful English village today. Some of these moats follow the pattern of continuing settlement on previously well used historic sites. In Bedfordshire moats were dug at the sites of monastic farms at Yarl's Wood, founded by Caudwell Priory, and at Houghton Conquest, on land previously farmed by Chicksands Abbey. At Ruxox, close to Flitwick, the moat was dug on Dunstable Priory land previously used by retired nuns. At Bolnhurst the moat was dug into the edge of a former Iron Age fort, underlining the human tendency to remain settled on one site. The recording of a drowning of a man in the moat at Birchfield Farm, Great Barford, in 1205 showed these water-filled ditches were not risk-free, however.

Up to the end of the thirteenth century, the rural economy experienced a period of growth aided by a benign weather pattern. The open field system was not yet under pressure and while ambitious landlords had begun to enclose small, irregular fields, this caused no massive social upheaval. However, in the second half of the fourteenth century, life began to unravel for many people in rural villages and the growing market towns. The Domesday Book provided a convenient baseline for the collection of taxes, which placed a heavy burden on landowners, who in turn passed this on to the common people. People must have had some security concerns, which required the ongoing occupation of motte and bailey castles and the construction of moated farmsteads. The prominent motte and bailey castle at Cainhoe, Clophill, was abandoned by 1374, signalling a withdrawal of any security presence in the countryside. Life was precarious: the church levied a tithe, seed needed to be saved, and the millers paid. A few years of poor harvests could tip the countryside into despair – and, ultimately, revolt. The severe forest laws prevented the poor from using the resources of the countryside to the full, and this restriction was resented. Jean Froisset, described as a chronicler, who was an official historian to the royal court, summed up the increasing fragility and uncertainty of rural life:

'This they would no longer bear, but had determined to be free, and if they laboured or did any other works for their lords, they would be paid for it.'

The stage was set for the arrival of the plague.

CHAPTER 6

THINGS FALL APART – PLAGUE, FAMINE AND COLLAPSE (1300–1750)

'There was in those days death without sorrow, marriage without affection, self-imposed penance, want without poverty, and flight without escape.'

John of Redding, 1300s

The landscape and rhythm of rural life at the time of the Domesday Book was to continue throughout the relatively prosperous twelfth century, with increased security at the expense of more feudal laws and serfdom. Henry I simply reassigned large tracts of land to the Norman elite, who reserved land to be worked as part of their estate (or 'demesne') and required the remainder to be worked by peasant farmers in the open fields, as introduced by the Saxons.

Estimates show a rapid rise in population from the time of the Domesday Book until the early fourteenth century, as the Norman rule secured peace and the climate was stable. There were moves to expand into what was termed 'waste land' (where the common people could graze livestock) and the small-scale enclosure of land continued. Expansionary religious houses were granted land by the large estates, and began to move towards a form of commercial agriculture. These establishments were increasingly pampered by 'gifts of faith' by landlords: Bushmead Priory is an example of land being gifted, then enclosed. In the south of the county, sheep grazing on the chalk downs became more intensive, with religious houses such as Dunstable Priory owning large flocks.

However, almost imperceptibly, beginning around 1315, rural life began to unravel. The box overleaf describes the oscillations in climate which impacted on rural life. Harvests became unreliable when the temperature cooled by a degree or more: summers became cooler and wetter, and winters longer and colder. Thus began the Little Ice Age. This was linked to famines in the

Warmer or colder? Vineyards and frost fairs

A recurring theme throughout this book is the influence of the weather on the farmers and agriculture of southern England. In the context of climatic change, historic climate trends have become the subject of much scientific debate. Any attempt to explain patterns of land use, the crops grown, the food and drink produced, and outbreaks of disease can only be fully understood with an understanding of the climate at the time. Direct and reliable measurements of daily weather events have only been available since the nineteenth century, and therefore longer-term climatic conditions need to be reconstructed with the help of historical documents. These include historical records of diet, the length of growing seasons, and the duration of ice cover, together with other indirect measures of climate. Other more scientific approaches to seasonal measurement include tree rings, ice cores and sediment cores.

The climatic oscillation which made it possible to grow vines in southern and central England, and which climaxed during the Roman occupation of Britain, is known by historians as the Roman Climatic Optimum. In the absence of real weather records, the facts around this weather window are even more speculative. This warmer period was estimated as 150 BC to AD 400, after which the climate cooled until a return to warmer conditions around AD 900.

It is frequently pointed out that this was a prosperous time in European history. It coincided with Viking exploration of the New World, the founding of Norse settlements in Iceland and Greenland, and increased agricultural productivity and crop diversity in northern Europe. Interpreting the records of bountiful harvests over much of Europe has pointed to the region benefiting from a series of extended summers and mild winters. As proof of warmer average temperatures in northern Europe, scientists cite the existence of wheat cultivation and vineyards in areas that would not support these crops today.

Studies suggest that climatic patterns during the Middle Ages in Europe also resulted in several multiyear stretches of relatively pleasant conditions and reliable weather. This Medieval Warm Period (MWP), is thought to have lasted from approximately 900 to 1300 AD . The climate deterioration that followed the MWP led to a period known by historians as the Little Ice Age, in the mid-seventeenth century, and historical accounts now allow a direct correlation with recorded events, such as frost fairs. However, the impact of the climate on the agriculture and farm economy was dire.

The Little Ice Age brought colder winters to Europe – canals and rivers in England and Holland were frequently frozen deeply enough to support ice skating and winter festivals. The first River Thames frost fair was in 1607 and the last in 1814: later changes to the bridges and the addition of an embankment affected the river's flow and depth, diminishing the possibility of freezes. The winter of 1794–95 was particularly harsh.

A few scientists have attempted to assign a specific value to changes in average global temperatures. In 1965 the British climatologist Horace Lamb examined historical records of harvests and rainfall, along with tree ring data, and concluded that the MWP was probably 1–2°C warmer than early twentieth-century conditions in Europe.

fourteenth century. As with previous climatic fluctuations, such as the period of higher temperatures during the Roman occupation, the climate began to exercise a powerful influence on agriculture, rural life, and livelihoods. By the early 1300s, heavier rains and a cooling of the summers led to crop failures becoming increasingly common. There are records of a collapse in the ratio of seed corn sown to the amount harvested – from a return of seven times at the height of the warmer climate to a meagre return which barely left adequate seed to be saved for the following year.

The year 1315 is often taken as the end of the MWP, with a particularly wet spell marked by depressed harvests lasting until 1321. Climate scientists have named this six-year period the Dantean anomaly; Dante died in 1321. This period of disturbed climate was widespread across Europe. A monk at St Albans Abbey noted that 'the grain was not nourished by the warmth of summer sunshine'. The year 1316 saw the height of a famine in Europe which led to disease, the spread of crime, and even infanticide and cannibalism. In England, livestock – the bedrock of the rural economy – suffered, and a 'murrain' – an unspecified disease – killed animals, as it had throughout Europe. In Northampton, thirty-three prisoners starved to death. Poor weather led to bad health generally, with intestinal diseases becoming common from eating contaminated foods: this became a cycle as periodic famines led to a weakened population who were more vulnerable to disease. It is argued that this extended period of famine led to a significant increase in deaths and weakened a generation which would later succumb to the plague.

The Hundred Years' War with France from 1337 added pressure on resources, and this was made worse by a punitive tax regime based on the comprehensive record-keeping of the Domesday Book commissioners. In Bedfordshire we know that the tax base in 1377 was 20,337 households – that is, those who were counted as due to pay – but by 1381 this had fallen to 14,895. A detailed account of decline was written by Joyce Godber.[4] Villages such as Bolnhurst, Pertenhall, Keysoe and Riseley all complained that they were being taxed unfairly. It is interesting that these villages are all located on the colder upland clays north of the Great Ouse, where wetter years had a real impact on farming.

Men were called up to serve in the Hundred Years' War from 1337 onwards. This meant a shortage of workers to bring in the harvest. Land is recorded as uncultivated at Eaton Bray, Totternhoe and Barton. At Houghton Regis the explanation given was the poverty of the people, who had neither animals to plough nor seed to sow. In the second half of the fourteenth century, around 2000 acres were left uncultivated in Bedfordshire and more than twice that in Cambridgeshire. There seemed to be a spirit of hopelessness – or in some cases rebellion – in the countryside. A sermon by John Wycliffe in 1381 contained a passage which was close to sedition: 'Lords do wrong the poor man by unreasonable taxes. The poor perish from hunger and thirst and cold. In this manner the lords eat and drink the poor man's flesh and blood.'

These feelings of unrest led to the Peasants' Revolt of 1381, during which there were uprisings all across England. This was fuelled by a 1351 law that tried to cap wages in the face of an increasing shortage of labour. Local unrest was recorded in Dunstable over a market charter, and in Willington land rents seem to have been withheld by tenants for a decade from 1382. The countryside, which had hummed with activity in the twelfth and thirteenth centuries, was suffering – and was about to receive a knockout blow.

Calamity arrived in England from Europe, where the plague had spread rapidly in only two years from an eastern source thought to be the Crimea. In 1348 reports of 'pestilence' along the south coast of England were noted. During that same year, London was reported as being seized by ten months of terror. This was the

---

[4] See Joyce Godber (1984) *History of Bedfordshire,*Bedfordshire County Council, page 121. Godber illustrates the situation by showing declining tax returns in towns such as Leighton, Biggleswade and Dunstable.

beginning of numerous eruptions of disease throughout the fourteenth century (and plague in various forms was still regarded as a threat in the mid-1600s). The peak of the plague (or Black Death) in Bedfordshire was in 1349: it mostly affected people living in the towns. As the plague was passed on by coughing and sneezing, the crowded urban conditions proved to be ideal for rapid infection.

In rural areas of Bedfordshire the impact of the plague may not have been so great, or perhaps was not recorded, and therefore it's difficult to ascertain how many villages were deserted due to the plague alone. It was more common for a number of factors to come together to make a village site no longer viable. From the Saxon period to the beginning of the fourteenth century, the swelling population had led to new villages in locations which were tenable when the climate was favourable. However, at other times this land was at best marginal, and villages in Bedfordshire that had expanded on to less amenable clay soils, especially in the north of the county, found that the higher rainfall meant that the cold, wet land in the spring was more difficult to cultivate. These acres usually fell back into pasture. A series of poor harvests around 1316 were especially damaging.

One reason that often tipped a village over the brink into abandonment was the death of the priest – an essential part of a rural parish. Joyce Godber charts deaths among the clergy: in her account, priests died at Chalgrave, Eaton Socon, Silsoe and Toddington and in some places the replacement priest also died. In Bedfordshire, fifty-four priests died in 1349 alone. It is important to emphasise the central role of the church within a village at this time. Parish priests were literate, when the vast majority of the population was not, and therefore played a central role in civil and religious life. The importance of visual imagery in a non-literate society is well illustrated by the intriguing remnants of thirteenth-century wall paintings depicting Biblical scenes, now unfortunately mutilated, which were once the focal point of Chalgrave Church.

Living in the manor house was not safe either. At Clophill the lord died, followed by his son two months later, and there were no rents paid, 'as all were dead from the pestilence'. Rural life was disrupted in other essential ways: in 1351 Riseley was recorded as having 300 acres of arable land uncultivated as 'no one wants to occupy them', and at Pavenham the mill closed as there was no miller. At Haynes the windmill had broken down and was unused in 1376. In 1361–62 there was another outbreak of the plague. The level of rural population hanging on to life and living a marginal existence is illustrated at Bolnhurst in the north of the county, where there were some 900 deaths. This high mortality rate implies a density of population far in excess of the current level. In contrast, Bolnhurst (reported with Keysoe parish in the 2011 Census) had a population of around 750. The implication is that in the mid-fourteenth century the population was many times this level. We do not know how many people died of the plague, but upper estimates suggest that half the rural population died. In Bedfordshire, around a third of the population succumbed.

The poor general health and sanitation of rural dwellers was obviously a major factor in the spread of the disease across the countryside, and these conditions prevailed into the fifteenth century. Another affliction, known as sweating sickness, was a mysterious, highly contagious disease that struck England, then Europe, in a series of epidemics beginning in 1485. The onset of symptoms was dramatic and sudden, with death often occurring within hours. The last outbreak occurred in 1551, after which the disease apparently vanished. However, malaria, or a form of malarial fever known as the ague, was still present. This weakened people, and the ague was most common in low-lying areas of Bedfordshire such as Flitwick Moor. The damp air of the moor was thought to be a cause of fever. A tree known as the Beaumont tree close to the village of Flitton was believed to have powers of protection against the ague. The prophylaxis was complicated, and included nailing strands of hair to the tree, a practice that continued into the eighteenth century.

In cities, where more people lived in close proximity, epidemics spread quickly. This was made worse as trade grew, bringing strangers into the mix, whereas in rural areas the uncertain climate and its impact on farming was the main factor, providing an environment where disease could spread rapidly. Climatic disruption runs like a thread through this period. An example is the Great Storm of 1322, which brought down the tower of Ely Cathedral, which was later replaced by the much admired lantern, using wood from the ancient abbey lands at Chicksands.

The role of ancient woodlands during the medieval period was vital in sustaining livelihoods, allowing a hard-pressed rural

How old is that wood?

Ancient woodland and plantations

In 1664 John Evelyn (1620–1706) published the first known book on English forestry. His *Sylva – A Discourse of Forest Trees and the Propagation of Timber* became so popular that it was reprinted four times during his lifetime and many times after his death. This was the first time any attention had been paid to planting trees, rather than cutting woodland for more agricultural land. The motive behind the publication is contained in the second part of its title: the need to produce timber, mainly for the navy. Since John Evelyn raised this issue, many other people have shared his concern – following the Napoleonic wars, and again much later in 1919 and in 1945 after the depletion of woodland during both world wars. At the same time, reliable maps began to be produced, mapping out the country's forests as well as much else. If a wood existed and was recorded in 1600, it is now regarded as an ancient wood.

These ancient woodlands are important historically and scientifically as they contain communities of plants that are now rare; they have undisturbed soils which are of interest; they often contain interesting manmade features such as medieval boundary markers and charcoal burning sites; and, most importantly, they are valued by the public and are beautiful places. Bluebells in the spring and abundant fungi in the autumn are common sights. Maulden Wood is an example of an ancient forest.

In Bedfordshire, overall woodland is estimated at about 7 per cent, of which 1500 hectares could be regarded as ancient. All these woods are designated as Sites of Special Scientific Interest (SSSIs).

population access to additional resources. A brief explanation of how woodlands are defined as 'ancient' is provided above. The steady decline in woodland as the larger estates converted waste land and woods to usable land began to impact on the rural economy, however, and the subsequent loss of tree cover in the following centuries reduced the woodland reserves that could be used in times of crisis.

By the beginning of the twentieth century, England was the least wooded landscape in Europe. The survival of ancient woods is now viewed as an important national asset recognised by legal designations including SSSIs (such as Maulden Wood, Swineshead and Odell Great Wood).

The collapse of rural life and the consequent rural social upheaval has been explained by the coming together of several factors. Soil exhaustion, where the addition of manure as fertiliser could not keep pace with the increased pressure of cropping to feed a growing population, certainly contributed, and the change in climate, leading to less favourable growing conditions, didn't help. Add the arrival of disease, the cost and disruption of the war with France, a harsh tax regime, and the system was brought to the edge of collapse. There seemed to be some recovery in the rural economy towards the end of the fourteenth century, and this social upheaval brought to the surface some winners as well as the many thousands who lost everything, or died. Labour costs were now twice the pre-plague levels, and a shift was emerging in the balance of power between peasants and landowners. This is best illustrated by the depletion of monks and lay brothers listed at the various ecclesiastical sites in the county. At Warden Abbey, a substantial Cistercian monastery, only twenty-four monks and six lay brothers were named in the tax return of 1379. This is a significant reduction from the estimated 65 monks and over 200 lay brothers who made up this religious community during the early thirteenth century. At Beadlow there remained only two monks and a prior. This would have meant that the busy farm on the grange lands held by these houses was impossible to maintain, and these farms began to pass to local landlords.

This change in the pattern of landholdings speeded up following the dissolution of the monasteries from 1536 to 1541. Land owned by monasteries was either granted to members of the gentry for services rendered to the king, or purchased by members of the gentry. At this time, the merchant class had the opportunity to acquire land and build on it a large country house and surrounding park. Many of the estates established in the post-medieval period are still in private hands. Evidence of the thriving rural economy fostered by these monastic houses survives, however, in the present landscape. Features such as fishponds, wildfowl lakes, rabbit warrens and mill sites can be traced back to an association with a manorial or religious establishment. The dissolution process was overseen by the Court of Augmentations, and county records provide an intriguing glimpse into monastic finances.

Social historians have characterised this period as one of the great levellers in society, moving the demand for labour to the centre and delivering more economic leverage to the people. The drive to 'improve' land, drain wet patches and enclose common land was gathering pace, as new landowners looked for profits and realised the limitations of the feudal farming system. In Bedfordshire, as we will see, this resulted in one of the most important changes and led to the creation of the iconic estate landscapes which are now a feature of the county.

CHAPTER 7

IMPROVING ON NATURE – GARDENS, PARKS, FARMS AND WOODS (1700–1850)

Any account of landscape history needs to take account of the accelerating speed of landscape change as the population increases and technology advances. The century from 1760, when George III (also known as Farmer George) came to the throne, until the arrival of the steam railway saw a huge change in rural life and the shape of the countryside. This was for a number of reasons. Within this period the enclosure of land transformed the layout of the countryside and the parkland estates in Bedfordshire, which became one of the most recognisable landscape features of the county, were enhanced. Country houses were built with formal planned gardens and extensive parks, and capital invested into farms and the land.

This period is therefore difficult to parcel into a neat chronology, as strands overlap and intertwine. For example, in Bedfordshire the growth of the market gardening industry was evident by the early 1700s, but required the advent of the railway to reach large urban markets in the mid-nineteenth century. In a similar way, the attention paid to formal gardens and parklands was given impetus by the enclosure of land, which enabled greater productivity – and therefore revenue – from agriculture. Therefore this chapter mainly deals with the evolution of what is often described as the 'picturesque landscape' movement and the significant impact it had on Bedfordshire, especially on its historic parklands and gardens. Chapter 8 goes on to discuss the changes in the farming landscape which have given us the familiar countryside we see today.

Bedfordshire is blessed with estates and great parklands. Today we tend to see these as separate elements – a grand house, gardens, a park, and surrounding farmland. However, this separation would have been foreign to the landowners who commissioned landscape designers such as Capability Brown or Humphry Repton. They conceived their parks as a whole – house/garden/park/farm – and they were designed to be enjoyed as such. Today we can recognise and value these parklands as an important part of the leisure and tourist industry – for example, Woburn, Wrest Park and Luton Hoo. We have also inherited wonderful public spaces close to towns – such as at Ampthill and Flitwick. However, the farmland aspect has been absorbed into the general pattern of agriculture throughout the county, and the history of these fields can now only be seen in a clump of trees or the relic of a former pond.

The gardens and parklands

The great parklands of Bedfordshire, such as Woburn, are often seen as representative of all that is typical in the English countryside. They are certainly now valued by the valued by both local users and visitors and regarded as integral to the landscape. They may include open, grazed land providing extensive views, studded with isolated ancient trees or strategically sited clumps of trees, and often with additional landscape features to delight the eye, such as avenues, lakes or ponds, and the occasional folly. These parklands have evolved from a variety of origins, and it is possible to separate out a number of distinct phases in this evolution and relate these to what we see today.

In Bedfordshire we are fortunate to have examples of very old enclosed parks, as well as others with a shorter history. The practice of emparkment became a notable feature of the medieval landscape, and the verb 'to empark' is recorded as early as 1334. However, the parks which are best known today are associated with the larger and grander houses in Bedfordshire and are most extensive and striking in the centre of the county along the Greensand Ridge. There are estimated to be some thirty parks, or remnants of parks, which can still be identified.

The reason for this is partly the location of medieval monastic houses in this area which, after the dissolution of the monasteries, became the centre of new aristocratic estates: for example, at Woburn and Chicksands. The creation of parklands was usually associated with the drive, enthusiasm and money of a few individuals who wanted to create a unique landscape. In Bedfordshire people such as the 6th Duke of Bedford at Woburn and Lord Ossory at Ampthill spent considerable fortunes employing celebrated landscape designers and architects.

The Bedfordshire estates: the evolution of parkland

The abundance of parkland and open countryside associated with large estates is a feature of Bedfordshire, especially along the Greensand Ridge. It is possible to trace the history of these distinctive areas of countryside.

Ecclesiastical houses (post-1066)

As we have seen from the Domesday Book records, the church was a major landowner in medieval England: land was often gifted to the church by wealthy patrons hoping to gain heavenly advantage. The less favourable land of the Greensand Ridge attracted the development of a number of monastic communities, including Warden Abbey and Chicksands Priory.

Deer parks (1000 to the 1600s)

This period saw a proliferation of deer parks, which were introduced to facilitate the Norman love of hunting. Deer parks reached their heyday in the 1300s and by the early seventeenth century many had been transformed into the recognisable parkland landscapes we have today, such as Battlesden and Ampthill.

Formal parks (1600s–1700s)

The seventeenth-century fashion for aristocratic landowners to send their sons on a Grand Tour of Europe ushered in a new phase of grandeur in landscape design, with influences from France, Italy and the Netherlands. The exposure to continental design and ideas made an impression on these young minds, and returning travellers were keen to rethink their estates. Parks were no longer seen as separate to the house to which they belonged, and it became fashionable to connect a house and the countryside around by ensuring you could enjoy wonderful views from the house, such as at Southill Park. Typical features of this period include tree-lined avenues, formal lakes, pavilions, entrance lodges and plantations.

The landscape park (1700 to early 1800s)

An English style of parkland design then developed, in which Capability Brown became the key figure. His approach was to simplify the estate and make it appear as informal as possible. Capability Brown included Ampthill (Figure 7.1), Haynes, Southill and Luton Hoo within his portfolio, while Battlesden, The Hazells at Sandy, Woburn and Moggerhanger were influenced by Humphry Repton.

Victorian parkland (mid-1800s to early 1900s)

This period saw the introduction of horticultural periodicals and an interest in plant collecting, especially trees. Collectors sponsored by wealthy landowners brought new species back to the UK from all over the globe. Arboreta became fashionable and were added to many estates, such as Flitwick Manor, and exotic trees were planted at Wrest Park and Woburn (Figure 7.2). Putteridge Bury House was rebuilt in 1911 after a fire, and the garden was remodelled by Gertrude Jekyll, an outstanding gardener at the time.

Figure 7.1. Ampthill House and Park from the Greensand Ridge. The elevated sandstone escarpment which runs through Ampthill Great Park offers views across the Oxford Clay Plain. During 2015, Ampthill Town Council, assisted by the Heritage Lottery Fund, embarked on the clearance of scrub and some trees from the steep scarp slope, with the goal of opening up the views and allowing a view of the house which would have been close to the view intended by Capability Brown. (Photograph by the author.)

The most significant changes have been engineered by the combination of an influential, affluent estate owner, an outstanding gardener and a skilled landscape designer. This is at the heart of the Bedfordshire story. One of the best known English gardeners, Capability Brown, worked extensively in the county.

Figure 7.2. The impressive cedar of Lebanon at Woburn. Throughout Bedfordshire, exotic trees such as this lend additional character to the landscape. Many of these outstanding landscape trees are recorded in *Champion Trees of Bedfordshire* by David Alderman and Pamela Stevenson. (Photograph by the author.)

The gardeners of Bedfordshire: Capability Brown

Lancelot Brown was born in Northumberland, the second son of a well-established farming family. He is believed to have been involved with around 260 sites in England during his career, of which 150 still exist. Bedfordshire is well represented, with documented work carried out by Brown at Ampthill Great Park, Luton Hoo and Southill. Wimpole Hall in Cambridgeshire is of special interest: it was inherited by the de Grey family in 1764, who were then living at Wrest Park, Silsoe. Jemima de Grey (1723–97) met Brown during his extensive commissions at Wimpole, and she invited him to work on the Wrest Park Estate in 1748. However, his impact at Wrest was relatively limited as Jemima was aware of the legacy Brown had left at Stowe, and confined any radical changes he made at Wrest to the edges of the park: she considered the formal parterres and lakes to be worth preserving and wished to retain what she described as 'the mystery of the gardens' (Hann and Garland, 2011). This juxtaposition of her and Brown's ideas resulted in a fascinating garden history at Wrest, with the existing canals softened by Brown and contrasting with the formal gardens still visible from the terrace of the present house.

These gardens were inspired by a previous owner on his return from the European Grand Tour: Henry de Grey imported his garden ideas from the Low Countries and Italy. The formal European garden style was fashionable from around 1650 until 1740, when this trend was upended by a new generation of gardeners. Lady de Grey recognised the talent Capability Brown had to visualise a landscape, and she understood that while the elements of his design were all pre-existing in the land, 'his touch has brought these out' (Hann and Garland, 2011).

It is important to remember that Brown never worked on a blank canvas. He was often required to amend and improve land in order to make existing parks and gardens more fashionable. This was long-term work, and he did not live to see the trees he planted come to their full glory.

Brown's genius lay in his ability to recognise, and make the most of, the 'capabilities' within a landscape, and he used this term in his engagement with his clients. The addition of Capability to his name reflected his sales technique, which flattered the client by remarking on the inherent 'capabilities' of the client's estate, implying Brown was the man to fully demonstrate and display these in his designs. This is what would today be described as his 'unique selling point'. His work has been described as taking a light rubber to the landscape and blurring the edges. Others were more critical of him: one remarked that Brown 'had not left an acre of shade and not three trees in a line from Land's End to the Tweed' (Brown, 2011). He has been considered both a visionary and a vandal, but he was undeniably a great networker, going from rich client to even wealthier landowner, continually on the move.

Lord and Lady Ossory at Ampthill also wanted a more fashionable garden. What was seen to be a desirable landscape had changed radically since the garden at Ampthill House had been set out under the direction of Lord Ashburnham following his European Grand Tour. The Ossorys were left with a legacy of formality: parterres and terraces, fountains and ponds. This was the opposite of what was seen as progressive and fashionable. Capability Brown was invited to reshape Ampthill Park in 1772 for a fee of £2396, and his stamp on the landscape is still evident today. Here, as elsewhere in Bedfordshire, the Brown technique was to create signature features or 'eye-catchers', including avenues, ponds and tree clumps on the ridge above Ampthill. His understanding of landscape can be seen in the Great Park, where he created a small lake and dammed a number of ponds using the outflow from the spring line where the permeable Greensand rock meets the impermeable Oxford Clay.

At other sites he created lakes to reflect an image of the house in the water, although in Ampthill the topography made this impossible. This work was naturally expensive. Brown was commissioned to work on the Southill Estate in the 1770s. By 1777 the work was complete. However, the work had cost more than anticipated and by 1795 the estate had been sold. The new owners complained about mortar 'left ready to be used and piles of tottering bricks'.

Brown became the landscape gardener of choice for the redesign and modernisation of great estates and gardens, where money was no object. In this he was greatly aided by the rising tide of imported tree species, notably Lebanon cedars, which grace many of his gardens. The introduction of cedars to England took place in 1742, and the wonderful examples at Southill were planted by Brown during his spells at the estate in 1764 or 1775–77. The archive at Southill contains accounts from Brown for this period, but no record of payment before his death in 1783 is preserved.

Humphry Repton adds a 'degree of magnificence'

As mentioned earlier, the title of this book comes from a quotation by Humphry Repton, who acted as a consultant to landowners, in contrast to Brown, who acted as a contractor. Brown shifted hills and dug canals. Repton coined the phrase 'landscape gardener' and was always anxious to work not only with the estate owner but also, and importantly, the wife of the client. He diligently consulted landowners, providing them with beautifully illustrated books with red leather covers. These became known as 'Red Books', and they laid out a vision of what Repton advised. He specialised in designing picturesque gardens which could be enjoyed by the owners and visitors on a number of levels. The large, handsome volumes of paintings were modern in concept: they contained a painting by Repton of the existing view accompanied by a hinged overlay that showed his vision for the land. This 'before and after' treatment can be compared to how a modern garden planner works, with a digitally produced, enticing picture of what could be achieved, given a flexible budget. The Repton philosophy attempted to 'animate a landscape' – he wanted to create a pleasure garden where the visitor would encounter a number of experiences. Woburn still has a 'pleasure dairy', strangely designed in a Chinese style, where the Duchess and her guests could indulge in cheese-making. This building was to be approached by boat across a newly constructed lake, adding to the experience. He said of his improvements to Barningham Hall in Norfolk: 'The following three principles, however much they may be in variance with each other, have all been considered in the plan here suggested: first, economy; second, convenience; and third, a certain degree of magnificence. These have been placed according to the respective weight each bears in my mind' (Louden, 1840).

The contrast between Repton and Brown is well illustrated by the gardens at Woburn. Capability Brown certainly visited the estate at Woburn, but there is no evidence that he was given a commission there. Repton, in contrast, imposed his characteristic stamp on the estate, and his Red Books provide a clear record of what he proposed. The resulting landscape and garden was mapped by Jeffery Wyattville in 1838, and this plan is still used by the present Duke of Bedford to guide changes to the garden. The idea is to bring the garden back to – or as close as possible to – Repton's vision. Indeed, if you visit the gardens today, you will be given a copy of this 1838 map.

As mentioned above, Repton's approach was that of a consultant making a pitch to his clients, and he backed up his ideas with lavish illustrations. Some of his clients represented new money, so appearances were very important, and Repton understood his market. He wanted his ideas to appeal to all the household, and he also recognised the need for economy in running a large estate. Hence he wanted to create a park that was profitable and had grazing for animals in a pre-tractor farming system; he wanted to ensure the convenience of a well-designed house and garden to appeal to the mistress; and not to be overlooked was his central idea that the house and garden had to impress – to have 'a certain degree of magnificence'. What was implied in this final requirement was the addition of something which today we might call the 'wow factor'. While the essence of Repton's approach was to improve the natural scenery and make the whole appear as natural as possible, he made sure the house and gardens were given pre-eminence.

Repton's work at Moggerhanger Park is a good example of his approach. He worked there in 1792, completing a Red Book, and was commissioned again in 1797. He was rather sniffy about the house, noting it was too ornamental for a farmhouse, too humble for a family country seat, too far from London to be called a villa, and should be described as an occasional sporting seat. He also fussed about the layout, remarking that there was difficulty in the management of the view from the drawing room and this room was exposed to the occasional defilement of horses waiting at the front door. His distinctive mark on the landscape design is also found at The Hazells, close to Sandy, and at Wimpole Hall. There is a possibility he also worked at Battlesden Park.

There is no doubt that Repton became the darling of society – to the point where his talents were recognised by Jane Austen in *Mansfield Park*. However, his professional advice irritated some people: Lord Torrington of Southill notes in his diary, following a meeting with the great gardener:

'Mr Repton – the now noted landscape gardener – came in and delayed me for half an hour: he is a gentleman I have long known, and of so many words that he is not easily shaken off; he asserts so much, and assumes so much, as to make me irritable, for he is one [of the many] who is never wrong, and therefore why debate with him?'

Joseph Paxton

Although Paxton (1813–65) was born at Milton Bryan and began his career close by at Battlesden Park, his impact on the garden landscapes of Bedfordshire is limited. He did remodel Battlesden House later in his life, but in 1860 the estate was bought by the Duke of Bedford, who demolished the residence. There remains one lake, or large fish pond, on the estate, which is reputed to have been dug under Paxton's supervision when he was very young. Unfortunately, this is the only contribution made by the man who went on to design the Crystal Palace in 1851 (and become very rich, thanks to his business interests in the booming railway industry). The story has a neat finale in that the Paxton contribution to the new technology of glass-house gardening required an increased supply of vitreous sand, much of which came from the Heath and Reach quarry close to his birthplace.

Fashionable farming

During this period, it was also fashionable to build a 'model farm' – these were designed with aesthetics in mind, but also to achieve optimum efficiency. The ideal, as promoted by the landscape designers who set the fashion agenda, was to achieve an uninterrupted view from the great house to the garden, outwards to the landscaped park, and finally to a tidy and productive farmed countryside. As they did in many things, the Russell family led the way with Francis Russell, the 5th Duke of Bedford, creating a 'model farm' at Woburn. An essential element was attractive farm buildings, many of which have a distinctive E-shaped ground plan. The Woburn estate has a good example of this style.

Overall, the rural landscape was enhanced by many of these buildings, which are still evident today, including dovecotes, lock-ups, animal pounds, smithies, windmills, watermills and barns. Many were built of Bedfordshire brick. At Old Warden, Lord Ongley allowed his enthusiasm to spill over into the village beyond the park, where he built thatched cottages in a special style of local architecture known as 'cottage orne'.

Despite these fashionable notions, an important aspect of the era was the recognition that this was still a landscape where animals and horse-drawn transport were central, and therefore grazing and the conservation of hay for winter use was essential.

The duke and the drainer: Francis Russell and William Smith

The arguments advanced for enclosure by enthusiasts included the need to improve land and increase yields, and allow the breeding of improved livestock. Driven by the large landowners who had money, influence, access to new technology and substantial estates, the movement to sweep away the medieval open fields and enclose land became a powerful political force in the late eighteenth and early nineteenth century. This enthusiasm is well illustrated by the annual four-day-long Woburn Sheep Shearing held during the 1790s. The 5th Duke of Bedford, Francis Russell, was in the vanguard of agricultural improvement. He inaugurated the Woburn event, which was like a modern agricultural show and attracted interest throughout England and beyond, with visitors from Europe and the Americas. The gathering was much more than just a sheep shearing, and included ploughing and other competitions on which wagers could be placed. It also included the auction of wool from the large Woburn flock, as well as the sale of cattle. In the evenings, there were banquets and dances.

This sheep shearing event became *the* place to be seen, as it attracted London-based society figures as well as experienced farmers. The social whirl that surrounded this gathering is captured in a painting by George Garrard from 1804, *Woburn Sheepshearing,* which shows the duke surrounded by well-known society figures (who are helpfully numbered to aid recognition). They include the writer and agricultural reformer, Arthur Young, and to one side of the painting there is a figure named as William Smith, who is described as a drainer. William Smith went on to become known as 'Strata' Smith, and he is now hailed as the father of English geology. In 1815 he published the first comprehensive geology map of England, which is familiar to anyone who has lifted a geological hammer.

The attendance of William Smith at this event emphasises the way in which the Woburn event was perceived: it was an opportunity for what would today be described as networking. At this event Smith met the senior Woburn land steward, John Farey, who recommended Smith to Joseph Banks, then President of the Royal Society, as a useful person to advise on the drainage of lead mines in Derbyshire. Following this commission, Smith was invited to work for the Duke of Bedford to examine the possibility of draining land close to what is now Priestley Farm on the outskirts of Flitwick.

The need to improve agricultural production was behind the enthusiasm for draining land. Having a large wet area on his estate would have been an irritant to Francis Russell, and he would certainly not have invited visitors to view it. Today the farm is well known as a vegetable producer and retailer, with a local farm shop, but then it was surrounded by Prisley (now known as Priestley) Moor, a wet, ill-drained area that Smith successfully tackled. This work was clearly a success in agricultural terms, and Smith published a monograph about it in 1806. However, removing wetland areas from the landscape has downsides too: it removes an interesting ecological habitat from the landscape and contributes to the decline in wetland and wading bird species.

Hence the importance given by landscape designers to grassland, and the desire of the estate owners to improve what was often termed 'waste land'. This included the drainage of wet areas, where feasible.

The tree collectors

One of the essential components of Bedfordshire's parklands is trees – either striking single trees or small clumps. This feature was emphasised by the great wave of Victorian plant collection and the importation of exotic species to Britain. Throughout the county there were individual landowners who were passionate about woodland and who enhanced their estates by planting these new species. Flitwick Manor Park (to which there is free public access), now a small remnant of a much larger estate, still has outstanding examples of exotic trees. John Thomas Brooks (1784–1858) carried out extensive improvements throughout this estate and planted an arboretum. Wrest Park at Silsoe also benefited from this influx of new species, with its graceful, striking redwoods being the best examples. The arrival of the sequoia species or Wellingtonia redwoods around 1855 aroused public interest and added to the plant-hunting frenzy across the globe. Fine examples of these trees still grace the lawns at Wrest.

Landowners' desire to beautify the landscape and impress visitors was also driven by a commercial interest. There was growing concern over the state of the national timber supply, especially to the navy, and landowners were encouraged, or even shamed, into planting broadleaf species, specifically oaks. Receiving an income from the farmed land was also important; all the capital poured in to beautify the Bedfordshire estates would not have been possible without a substantial income from agricultural rents. However, these did not always bring in all the funds required to maintain an extensive estate, garden and country house, and (as mentioned above) the improvement of land became a driving force to improve income. The enclosure of estates was seen as essential in achieving improved agricultural productivity – and revenue. This enclosure of the former extensive open fields and common lands led to a social, as well as an agricultural, revolution, as we will see in the next chapter.

CHAPTER 8

WINNERS AND LOSERS – ENCLOSURE CHANGES THE LANDSCAPE (1700–1850)

'Thus came enclosure – ruin was its guide,
But freedom's cottage soon was thrust aside
And workhouse prisons raised upon the site.
E'en nature's dwellings far away from men,
The common heath, became the spoiler's prey;
The rabbit had nowhere to make his den
And labour's only cow was drove away.'

John Clare, *'The Fallen Elm'*

The decade from 1730–40 was especially brutal in the English countryside, as it coincided with a period of agricultural depression. However, a recovery around 1750 marked the beginning of a transformation in the rural economy. The countryside we see today was largely created in the century from 1740 onwards: over the course of that century, agricultural experiment and reform became the subject of national interest, agriculture became fashionable, capital was harnessed, and new energy drove reform forward. Parliamentary commissioners and land surveyors were appointed and made responsible for the enclosure of what remained of the open fields and common land.

The new landowners often realised, too late, that they were financially overcommitted: the cost of enclosing common land required substantial investments of capital, especially for hedging and drainage. Debts forced the sale of land, which began to pass down the social scale to enterprising individuals who spotted an opportunity and who could afford to buy the land. The scale of enclosure is best illustrated by the demand for hedging plants alone. An advertisement in the *Stamford Mercury* of 1824 asked for tenders from nurserymen to meet a demand for 30,000 ash tree saplings, and 500,000 hawthorn or 'quick-growing' plants. The urgency to enclose was being slowed by the shortage of materials to define the new boundaries.

I

Figure 8.1. The landscape after enclosure. This aerial photograph was taken in the 1950s, prior to the building of the city of Milton Keynes, and shows the rectangular hedged, ditched fields created by the enclosure movement. (Photograph from the archive of the Milton Keynes Development Authority.)

Enclosure – a quick guide

The **Enclosure (or Inclosure) Acts** were a series of **Acts** of Parliament that empowered landlords to **enclose** fields and common land in England and Wales. Enclosures were regulated by Parliament; a separate Act of Enclosure was required for each village that wished to enclose its land. Altogether 103 Bedfordshire parishes were enclosed by 95 Acts of Parliament, mostly during the late nineteenth century. In **1801**, Parliament passed a General Enclosure Act which enabled any village, where three-quarters of the landowners agreed, to enclose its land.

In the Middle Ages parishes consisted of three or more large common fields divided into open strips with no enclosing hedges, fences or walls. Each person might own a number of strips in various fields. In enclosure, commissioners working for the king surveyed the common fields, calculated the size of a peasant's landholding, assessed the quality of the land, and then allotted him a proportionate amount of consolidated acreage. The new entitlement was in one of the smaller fields that had been carved out of the former commonly worked land. The new fields were then enclosed by a hedge and ditch, or sometimes a fence. This new landscape gives us the modern pattern of regular fields we have today.

While the enclosure movement is often seen as a distinct historical period neatly defined by dates, the process had been slowly happening since Tudor times. There had always been local enclosures to keep sheep in, or cattle out of crops. These early enclosures were by private agreement and different in scale from the national wave of enclosure.

In Bedfordshire, significant dates in regard to this agricultural revolution were from 1740 to the late 1880s. Sutton Parish appears to have been the first to be enclosed, in 1741, and the last was Totternhoe, in 1886. Maps produced during the enclosure process show the location and ownership of individual strips of land that were to be enclosed, and the allocation of the new enclosed fields. The scale of these operations was a challenge to the surveyors who were recruited to map out the new landscape. At Thurleigh, eleven open fields were subdivided and enclosed in 1805: this land had been previously farmed from hamlets which have not survived. At Houghton Park Hall in south Bedfordshire, the map of 1772 clearly shows the pre-enclosure strips of individual holdings surrounding the imposing house. Maps of this type were required as part of the Enclosure Act, and would have been used by surveyors in enclosing the new individual holdings. These historic documents allow us a glimpse into a landscape that is long gone.

During this period, powerful landowners moved to enclose large areas quickly: twelve parishes in the Woburn Estate were enclosed between 1796 and 1817; the land owned by the Whitbread family was enclosed between 1800 and 1811; and land around Sandy and Everton was enclosed in 1804 under instruction of the Pym family. However, some landowners were in less of a hurry. At Biddenham the Act was passed in 1812, but it was not implemented until notice was formally given that enclosure of the common fields would take place by reading the proclamation at Divine Service on 10th October 1827.

The view from the country seat

Advocates for enclosing land marshalled a number of convincing economic arguments. The new farms were compact and therefore more efficient; there was a pressing need to revive old arable land which had been overcropped; and there was a great enthusiasm for progressive livestock breeding, which required the careful management of herds in separate fields. Following enclosure, the drive to improve the land gathered pace. Areas of wetland were reclaimed for agriculture; common land was enclosed; new crop rotations were introduced; improved equipment began to appear; and the cultivation of root crops was adopted. All of this was sound agricultural thinking, which recognised that the open fields could no longer support improved varieties of more intensive crops. From the sixteenth century onwards there was a preoccupation with soil improvement, and farmers added manure and lime to improve the soil. The search was on for new soil additives, without a real understanding of what best stimulated plant growth. The addition of coprolites was an early innovation. (See Lawes manure)

In Bedfordshire an insight into this thinking was provided by a survey carried out by William Stone in 1794. He reported that the county was very much neglected and farms managed by 'ignorant persons', and that livestock breeds were mixed on common land and sheep were of unprofitable quality. Some twenty-five parishes had been enclosed by this date, but the biggest changes were yet to come.

The consolidation of land into estates was a feature of the enclosure movement, and this enabled the new 'squires' to compete with the traditionally wealthy landed elite: in Bedfordshire, the Ongley family at Old Warden is a good example of this influx of new money and energy. The first squire was a London linen merchant who bought up parcels of land in the parish, creating what has been described as a 'very plentiful estate'. Remarkably, a record of his land dealing is preserved in a 'commonplace book' which contains copies of leases, land agreements, the names of tenants and even details of specific fields. The estate remained in the family after his death in 1726, and the marriage of Frances Burgoyne, to Robert Henley Ongley, 2nd Baron Ongley, in 1801 linked the estates at Southill (Ongley) and Sutton Park (Burgoyne) and further consolidated the family's landholdings. This allowed Robert Henley Ongley (1771–1814) to become 'an agricultural gentleman'. Ongley continued to enclose land and took an interest in all agricultural changes, including the Woburn agricultural events. He experimented with modernising farming equipment, introducing threshing machines.

Fertility and 'Lawes manure'

A major barrier to the enclosure movement was the requirement to improve soil fertility, long before artificial fertilisers were available. Livestock manure was finite, and the system of open grazing and large fields which were kept fallow for a season to restore fertility was seen as wasteful and at the root of the low productivity. The improving landlords were keen to introduce new crops, such as turnips, and more productive breeds of animal. The accidental discovery in Bedfordshire and Cambridgeshire that the addition of a geological deposit found at the base of the Greensand rocks improved plant growth came as a welcome boost to the booming agricultural industry.

These deposits, known as coprolites, are nodules of sediments deposited during the early Cretaceous period in a seaway that crossed Bedfordshire. The nodules were enriched by phosphates and formed concretions where the calcium carbonate was slowly replaced by phosphates. These deposits were mined across Bedfordshire, and workers moved in to villages such as Shillington, Potton and Arlesey.

Early scientific work at Cambridge University showed that these rocks had a high phosphate content, which is essential for the root systems of growing plants. In 1842, John Bennet Lawes took out a patent for the conversion of coprolites into what would become known as super-phosphate fertiliser, and a few years later a coprolite rush began. The new fertiliser became known as 'Lawes manure' or more simply as 'turnip manure'. Lawes, who owned a large estate at Rothamsted near Harpenden, set up a manure plant at Barking which was an immediate commercial success.

The Lawes Estate benefited from this endowment, and this led to the founding of the Rothamsted Agricultural Research Station, which was the first facility dedicated to agricultural science in the world. In 1843 Lawes set up long-term field experiments on this site to measures gains and losses in soil fertility; these experiments continue today on the same plots. Cambridge colleges also benefited from the economic upsurge, as did local landlords. The Lodge at Sandy was built partly with proceeds from the coprolite industry. The boom lasted until the late 1870s when imported phosphates from the Americas replaced locally produced ones. Prices fell from around £2 a ton to half this amount. Signs of this former major Bedfordshire industry are difficult to find today. At Potton, where there was at one time around 600 acres of workings, only shallow dips in fields remain to show where these workings once were.

His son, also confusingly called Robert Henley Ongley, took this landscape change further, laying out the Swiss Garden and remodelling the Old Warden village. This squire was the model of an improving landowner of the period, combining efficiency (in the consolidation of land parcels) with privacy and land improvement, and not forgetting to pay attention to fashion and impressing his peers.

In Bedfordshire, as elsewhere, enclosure meant that the remaining extensive open field system was replaced by a new layout of smaller rectangular fields and straight roads. Within the existing large country estates on the Greensand Ridge, and in particular those owned by the Dukes of Bedford, this large-scale reorganisation was undertaken by the estates themselves, without the need for parliamentary action. The 5th Duke began to apply more scientific methods of farming, and greatly expanded the property portfolio of the Woburn Estate. Within a decade the Bedfordshire Agricultural Society had been founded. Its first meeting was in The Swan Hotel in Bedford in 1801.

An early account of the approach pioneered by the 5th Duke comes from the agricultural writer and leading improver Arthur Young, who recorded many conversations with farmers at all levels of society. Young was especially impressed by the growing of carrots on more sandy soils around Woburn. However, he also came to acknowledge the negative aspects of enclosure, and his experience was sharpened by his visits to the Woburn Estate, where he saw first-hand the real hardship suffered by tenants, and he began to understand how enclosure had affected them.

The 5th Duke of Bedford emerged as one of the leaders of the agricultural revolution, using not only his considerable financial resources to improve his estates, but also his influence and connections. The extent of the national interest in agriculture at this time can be measured by the involvement of King George III. Adopting the pseudonym of Ralph Robinson, and referring to himself as 'an active farmer', he contributed to Arthur Young's *Annals of Agriculture* in the late 1700s. The king was commonly known as 'Farmer George', and became the founder and patron of the *Board for the Encouragement of Agriculture and Internal Improvement,* created by Royal Charter in 1793.

The king created what amounted to an experimental farm at Windsor and personally managed the Royal Forests and farms in

Surrey. In Bedfordshire the duke emulated this royal example by setting up experimental plots at Woburn. The interesting modern parallel here is that the internationally famous Rothamsted Research agricultural station still retains an experimental farm holding at Woburn in order to carry out scientific work on the sandy soils in this area of Bedfordshire, in contrast to the heavy land in Hertfordshire, where the research station is located.

Hortus gramineus Woburnensis:
How the grass grew at Woburn

The spirit of scientific enquiry which accompanied the agricultural advances at the end of the eighteenth century was mostly driven by the great landlords in England, and this is illustrated by experiments carried out at Woburn. George Sinclair, gardener to the 5th Duke of Bedford, set in train a long-running set of well-structured experiments on 242 plots, each 2 feet × 2 feet. His intention was to compare the productivity of different grass species and grass seed mixes across a range of soil types. His experimental plan was published in a book in 1816, *Hortus gramineus Woburnensis*, and the results are described in the third edition, published ten years later. His main conclusion seems to be that a greater diversity of plants in a plot leads to a larger overall weight of plant material: in other words, greater biodiversity increases productivity. The experimental result would have been of interest to the 5th Duke, especially in his pursuit of improved breeds and general livestock production. However, this pioneering work might have been overlooked had it not been for Charles Darwin noting these experiments in a few lines in *The Origin of the Species*, in which he argues that more diverse communities are generally more productive. This concept has become one of the fundamental rules of ecology – a science which, in the eighteenth century, while intuitively understood, had not yet been formalised. It could be argued that George Sinclair's Woburn experiments were the first field ecology trials worldwide.

All of this enthusiasm came from landowners. By the early 1800s, there was a belief that national prosperity could be created by means of an agricultural revolution and that this required state leadership to help increase agricultural yields and to integrate markets. This innovative thinking was driven by the rising population and the accompanying fear of food shortages at a time of national insecurity. One aspect of this transformation which marks the Bedfordshire landscape is the investment in brick-built model farms and substantial farm workers' cottages. This trend was started by the Russell family and other extensive landowners, such as the Howard and Whitbread families, followed.

The view from the cottage

Nationally there was a persuasive economic argument that the nation needed to bring the so called 'waste' or uncultivated land, together with common grazing, into production. The major landowners began to enclose common land, including rabbit warrens, poorly drained areas and rough grazing, to increase production. Along with these agronomic changes went sweeping social change and the removal of old practices, such as the payment of tithes to the church. The benefit to the general population was meant to be investments in infrastructure, such as improved drainage, better roads, and an inflow of capital. However, the most significant consequence of the enclosure movement was that land previously held in common, and that had been a mainstay of peasant livelihoods, was enclosed and the countryside became a network of rectangular fields hedged and ditched and, above all, privately owned. The experience of the people of Studham, south Bedfordshire, is typical, and shows the hardships they suffered by the removal of part of their common land, which had been a source of fuel and grazing. In 1870 landlords partly enclosed the common land to expand the existing estate holdings. This meant that people could no longer gather gorse (locally known as 'furze') to use as fuel. For the poorer cottagers this was the equivalent of removing modern income support, and gamekeepers on the estates were diligent in preventing the removal of any wood or fuel. These rights had existed in many cases in the form of an 'astover' (the right to gather fuel) since the Norman forest laws. The incentive offered for this loss was the improvement of local roads, but this was resented as the gravel for the road was taken from the remaining common land. The extent of the withdrawal of people's rights is illustrated in the wording of the acts. In Felmersham the title of the Act was: *'An Act dividing and enclosing the open fields, common pasture common meadow, and other commonable lands and grounds in the parish of Felmersham.'*

There is little doubt about the intention to privatise the common lands.

John Clare, the Northamptonshire poet, recognised that the resourceful peasant had all but disappeared from the rural landscape. Clare was savage in his commentary on the displacement of the poorest people. (See Chapter 12 for more on Clare's life.)

The speed of transformation is difficult to grasp. Nationally, between 1760 and 1815, some 4000 Acts of Parliament were passed. Widespread unrest followed, and there are records of minor revolts in Harrold and Flitton, and more significantly in Maulden (1796). The removal of rough grazing on land in the parish that bordered the River Flit and, more importantly, the withdrawal of the right to cut peat in the valley, led to some 200 villagers confronting the land surveyors sent to mark the new boundaries. A magistrate became involved and a riot was only avoided by the arrival of a mounted troop of soldiers quartered in Ampthill.

The sense of bitterness and betrayal was well shown at Bow Brickhill in Buckinghamshire, which was enclosed in 1790. Land was assigned to the rector in lieu of tithes, and the heathland was awarded to the 'poor of the parish', to be administered by trustees who were meant to manage this land for firewood collection and grazing. An inscription above the door of April Cottage in the village records what happened next: 'Bow Brickhill Heath was awarded to the poor of the parish in 1793. An Act of Parliament was obtained to sell it by the trustees!!! in 1844'. [The three exclamation marks are part of the original quotation.]

Nevertheless the enclosure movement rolled on. The diaries of writer and agricultural reformer Arthur Young show that he was moved by the plight of peasants. At Millbrook in 1800 he noted, *'These poor people know not by what tenure they hold their land; they say they once belonged to the duke but that duke has swapped them away to Lord Ossory. How little do the great know what they swop and what they receive.'*

The diary entry is more poignant since Young was on his way to meet the Duke of Bedford at Woburn, and the contrast between the Duke and the common people clearly disturbed him:

'Here is wealth and grandeur and worldly greatness; but I am sick of it as soon as I enter these splendid walls. I had rather be among the cottagers of Millbrook had I but the means of aiding them, but I will see Lord Ossory and try to do something for them.'

In neighbouring Northamptonshire there are also records from Haselbeck near Daventry, where empty crofts were mapped following enclosure. Some 700 acres of land which had previously been worked by cottagers had been enclosed. This, combined with the policy of raising rents, effectively led to the eviction of some sixty people who could not, or would not, pay. The other landowners in the parish may also have evicted tenants, and by 1897 all the common land had been enclosed.

The tenant farmer's view

From this period of upheaval emerged a growing class of tenant farmers with the skill and drive to farm profitably, and who were anxious to acquire land. However, they lacked adequate capital to purchase the areas of land required for a flourishing and cost-efficient country estate.

The rise of such forward-looking, energetic tenant farmers was made possible by the significant agricultural changes that had just taken place. Turnips first appeared in the probate records in England as early as 1638, but were not widely grown until about 1750. Turnips were recognised as an excellent forage crop – ruminant animals could eat their tops and roots through a large part of the year. As mentioned, the replenishment of the soil's fertility was a major concern of all farmers in this period, and by the 1870s guano and nitrates from South America were being applied. Thus there was less need for fields to lie fallow to allow the soil to recover. Changing to rotation farming made possible a crop succession: wheat to barley to turnips and finally clover in one field in successive years. Clover made excellent pasture, and growing it with turnips allowed more animals to be kept through the winter, maintaining soil fertility. In turn, this produced more milk, cheese, meat and manure. The area under wheat and barley rose during the nineteenth century, while rye dwindled to less than a tenth of its late medieval peak. Yields improved thanks to new and better seed, together with crop rotation, enhanced soil fertility, and machinery that had been designed to drill in rows. These overall improvements were made possible by long-term leases which allowed a class of small tenant farmers to become established. By 1850 tenant farmers formed a new, thriving entrepreneurial class, but the ownership of land remained solidly with the landlords. In 1850 around half of Bedfordshire was owned by only fifty people.

Thomas Batchelor and Robert Long: improving tenant farmers

Thomas Batchelor farmed at Lidlington as a tenant of the Woburn Estate. He was clearly an educated man and a leader in the movement to improve agriculture. He completed a survey of agriculture in Bedfordshire in 1807, and his comments on the use of machinery provide a snapshot of the take-up of new equipment such as seed drills. A drill sowing in straight lines was seen as a major advance over the previous use of broadcast sowing, and these drills were rare enough to be mentioned by Batchelor in his survey.

Some fifty years later, Robert Long farmed at Upper Stondon as a tenant of the Wrest Park Estate. He was also an educated man and kept a diary, which gives us a useful insight into the life of a progressive working tenant. Long used a steam engine and was obviously impressed by it, as he upgraded in 1863 to a more powerful machine. The dangers of this equipment are recorded in his journal when a worker suffered an unfortunate accident that led to the amputation of some of his fingers.

Long recognised the importance of fertilisers to improve soil quality, and bought horse manure and soot, which was in plentiful supply in London, to apply to his fields. Such was the energy of this farmer that he sought out new equipment and trends.

The beginnings of plantation forestry

Agricultural innovation was accompanied by a change in approach to other aspects of the rural landscape. In addition to beautifying their estates, landowners were conscious of the rising demand for timber, especially high-quality wood for ship building. New plantings were tried experimentally to assess whether it was worth using land for commercial forestry. The 5th Duke of Bedford oversaw, and even actively managed, tree planting in the Woburn Estate. A quote pinned to a noticeboard at the entrance to a Woburn wood illustrated his personal interest: 'This plantation has been thinned by John, Duke of Bedford, contrary to the advice and opinion of his gardener.'

One eloquent description of the grandeur of the Woburn Estate is from the diary of Daniel Defoe, who wrote about a visit in 1761. He was especially impressed by the great number of small roads through the woods 'whereby a Person may either walk or ride to every part of the park in the wettest Time, without meeting the least Dirt' (Defoe, 1978).

Heart of Oak, the British Bulwark

In the late eighteenth century there was growing concern over the supply of quality timber in England, especially oak for ship building. In 1649, Ampthill Park, then much larger than the present park, was estimated to have 400 oaks which were suitable for ships' timber. The great storm of November 1703, which lasted a week, felled a great swathe of woodland across southern England – and the concerns became a reality. This issue was the subject of a book by Roger Fisher published in 1763, entitled *Heart of Oak, the British Bulwark*. Fisher launched a crusade to encourage the great landowners of England to take forestry seriously and, above all, plant oaks. The Royal Society offered prizes for new plantings, and the dukes of Bedford led the way as model landowners. Fisher was unsparing in his criticism of his fellow landowners: 'Woods were destroyed by animals protected for the hunt, frittering away the birthright of future Britons to fund horses, dogs, wine, cards and folly.'

Roger Fisher found a kindred spirit in Thomas Johnes, who claimed to have planted 922,000 oaks. It is unclear if these were simply acorns or real saplings. Naval officers on leave were encouraged to take pockets full of acorns to country estates when on social visits. This was the period of 'oak mania'.

Modern foresters may smile at this, but there are serious issues facing broadleaf trees in contemporary Britain. Acute oak decline has been noted in several thousand trees across southern England

The 7th Duke of Bedford continued widespread tree planting, including on Cooper's Hill close to Ampthill, and his successors continued this tradition into the mid-nineteenth century, positioning the Bedford estate at the forefront of land management.

This era of improving landlords fired by a zeal to increase soil productivity, with ample capital and a keen sense of competition, eventually came to an end. Following a series of wet years in the 1870s which led to ruined harvests, and due to the beginning of regular imports of grain from North America thanks to free trade regulations, there were signs of a rural recession by 1886. Farms were left vacant and rural unemployment rose, with Potton especially badly affected, due to its large number of redundant coprolite miners.

However, the next phase of farming – harnessing the new steam technology – was just emerging. The next chapter discusses the part played by Bedfordshire in agricultural advancement, including the beginnings of the market garden industry and the scientific approach to modern agriculture taken at the Woburn experimental site and in agricultural engineering at Wrest Park.

CHAPTER 9

HIGH FARMING – BRICKS AND STEAM (1850–1914)

The period from 1850 to 1880 is often referred to by economic historians as the years of 'Victorian high farming' – when better prices and new techniques allowed confident, expansive investment in rural Britain. By 1851 the population balance had shifted, with more people living in towns and cities than in the countryside. The Industrial Revolution began this move of continuing urban growth from 1760 onwards, and this has never faltered since, despite a small increase in the populations of rural villages in recent decades. However, agricultural confidence ebbed away towards the close of the nineteenth century as the importation of cheaper grain and meat from the Americas began to affect demand, and prices fell. As sure as bust follows boom, the century ended with an agricultural depression.

An important thread running through this account of the landscape has been that the speed and scale of change increases over time, with a correspondingly greater visual impact. Technology usually explains this acceleration, but the sheer number of people involved is also a factor. This is well illustrated by the population rise in the first half of the nineteenth century, when numbers in England came close to doubling in fifty years.[5]

By 1850 there were already 6000 miles of railway in England. The impact of the railway was not confined to the new transport links and the growth of the major cities; even quiet rural communities had been opened up to the world beyond. The station clock became important as Standard Time arrived in the countryside. However, the most important development at this time in Bedfordshire was the emergence of large-scale market gardening. Navigation of the rivers Great Ouse and Ivel had improved in the late eighteenth century, stimulating the urban growth of Bedford and many of the smaller villages along the rivers. Brewing, malting, tanning, straw plaiting, hat making and agricultural engineering were all important industries that provided employment in

---

[5] The first national census was in 1801. In England the population was recorded as just short of 10 million. By 1851, it was almost 18 million.

Bedfordshire's towns. The railway boom in the middle of the nineteenth century was crucial to the development of these towns and to the growth of many industries, such as quarrying and brick-making, which required cheap transport to move sand, gravel, stone and bricks to service the demand for building materials in the expanding cities. The requirements of constructing the railways also further fuelled the demand for building materials. The steam engine revolutionised many of the industrial processes carried out in Bedfordshire's countryside, such as arable cultivation, threshing, and especially milling. More farm buildings began to be built of bricks and designed to accommodate steam engines, rather than horses.

The market gardens

While supermarkets today stock an impressive range of fresh and frozen vegetables sourced from across the globe, the connection of the humble Brussels sprout to Bedfordshire is firmly implanted in English food culture – there is even a named Bedford variety of sprout available to growers. The beginnings of this vegetable-growing industry reach back to at least 1610 when William Spring, described as 'a gardener from Sandy', was recorded as producing cabbage, carrots and turnips from a one-acre smallholding. This small-scale horticultural activity continued to prosper in the area for over the next two centuries, and was still very common in eastern Bedfordshire in the mid-nineteenth century. There is no evidence that parliamentary enclosures led to problems for independent gardeners. Indeed, in Sandy parliamentary enclosure allowed some gardeners to increase their acreage, with enterprising growers moving on to unenclosed land along the Ivel River terraces. During this period the financial turnover of many gardeners must have been quite considerable. Making a profit at a time when costs such as labour and rents were high, and returns depended on favourable weather and intensive seasonal effort, required both skill and luck.

The physical attributes of the land along the major rivers were central to the concentration of horticultural enterprises. As already noted, land along the Great Ouse and Ivel river terraces was valued from the Iron Age onwards. A combination of light, easily worked soils, on gentle slopes, close to a water supply which could be used for transport, to power grain mills and also for crude irrigation, was a winning combination. Today there is still a concentration of specialist horticultural growers along the lower slopes of the Greensand Ridge and on the terraces of the river valleys. Modern technology means irrigation from the rivers is still possible, if expensive, and the sight of overhead sprayers is common in summer. Some growers have diversified into the cultivation of roses, and others have exploited the central location of the area and the proximity of good transport links by becoming an essential part of the fresh vegetable supply chain.

Commercial gardening continued to grow steadily in popularity, and received a major boost with the construction of rail links in the mid-nineteenth century, so fresh vegetables could be transported to the London and Midlands markets. The Bedford–Hitchin line followed in 1857, which involved building the ambitious 800-metre (2625-feet) tunnel at Old Warden. There was also a reverse flow along these rail links: to enhance the light soils and add fertility and what growers referred to as 'body', various organic materials were returned to the soil, including a residue produced by the woollen industry (known as 'shoddy') from the north of England, and manure from London, most likely including night soil. Figure 9.1 shows the focus of the market gardening industry in the county.

Building in brick

Any account of the landscape in Bedfordshire should mention the importance of the extractive industries, especially the brick pits, but it should also note the impact of the chalk quarrying, sand extraction (around Leighton Buzzard), and the former Fuller's earth pits at Woburn Sands and Clophill. However, it was the demand for bricks in the nineteenth and twentieth centuries that made the greatest impact on the landscape, economy and social history of Bedfordshire.

The importance of the brick clays deposited on the chalk at places such as Caddington is referred to in earlier chapters. These pits yielded many prehistoric flint implements, and during the Victorian period the collection of these artefacts was very popular, with many local gentlemen amassing impressive displays of flints – which have made a significant contribution to our understanding of the past. Local brick-making has always been a feature of rural industry in Bedfordshire, and former clay pits are recorded in many

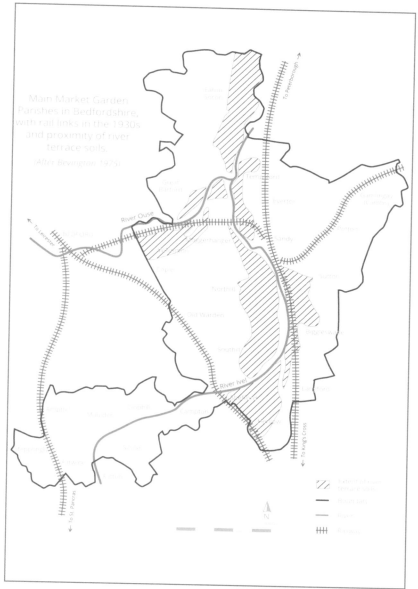

Figure 9.1. Market garden parishes in Bedfordshire. This figure illustrates the relationship between the flat and friable soils of the Ouse and Ivel river valleys and the Bedfordshire parishes that have a historic connection to the market gardening industry. The rail lines, which are also marked on the map, were completed in the mid-nineteenth century, forming a link to the urban markets. This relationship was described by Frank Beavington (1975). (This figure has been redrawn by John Hamley.)

villages today, or marked by street names such as Kiln Lane in Clophill. In an era when transport was expensive, the most sensible business model was based on local production to minimise transport costs.

More information about the brick-making industry in the Marston Vale can be found in Cox (1979) and Hillier (1981). The commercialisation of the industry began in the early 1880s when the Fletton Estate close to Peterborough was sold to a consortium of local brick-makers who were initially attracted by the local market for new houses in the area. Only when bricks were made and tested in trials at Fletton did these fortunate entrepreneurs discover that the Lower Oxford Clay had the unique ability to ignite when heated. Residual organic matter within the clay was ignited when it reached a certain temperature, allowing substantial savings in the fuel required to fire the bricks. This also led to more even heating and a stronger brick. Additionally, the moisture content of the clay made it easier to process. The Fletton Brick industry soon expanded into the Marston Vale. In 1897 a new commercial brick-making site was opened by B.J. Forder at Wooton Pillage on the Oxford Clay south of Bedford. This more efficient industry soon replaced the older brick-making sites on the less promising Gault Clays around Harlington and other sites in south Bedfordshire. The industry grew quickly to become, for a short time, the largest single brick-making site in the world. By the 1930s Bedfordshire had 162 brick chimneys and was producing around 500 million bricks per year. The chimneys became the most recognisable Bedfordshire landmark. In the later part of the twentieth century, technology and environmental regulations impacted on the industry and the major extraction and manufacturing works moved east to a site on similar geology around Peterborough.

After the clay pits were abandoned in the late twentieth century, they quickly filled with water. Together with the former brick-making plants, these were regarded as an unfortunate blight on the landscape, useful only for the disposal of London rubbish. More imaginative thinking turned this around, and the government initiative to create new public open spaces led to the creation of the Forest of Marston Vale country park on the former extraction site. The innovative Millennium Forest concept, backed by national and local government, had the long-term aim of enhancing the landscape by planting new woodlands. This provided scope for

Figure 9.2. Stewartby Lake in 1984, with the brick chimneys in operation. The large lake, now a home to wildlife and used for water sports, was then no more than a stretch of open water, dangerous to swim in, and known only to a few intrepid birdwatchers. In late 2017 there was an application to demolish the final four chimneys to make way for a housing development.[6] (Photograph by the author.)

landscape restoration, conservation, public engagement and education. In Bedfordshire the Forest of Marston Vale site quickly won public support thanks to creative ideas which drew in schools and local volunteers, and has rapidly become one of the most popular recreation locations in Bedfordshire.

Other former extraction sites have been transformed into valuable conservation locations. The digging of peat from Flitwick and Flitton moors left a legacy of water-filled areas which now form the core of a Site of Special Scientific Interest (SSSI) with an array of interesting plants as well as rare dragonflies and damselflies. Thomas Fisher, an artist who painted many Bedfordshire scenes, captured the extraction of peat in a painting dated around 1815.

---

[6] Bedford Borough Council approved the decision to demolish the remaining chimneys in January 2018. However, approval was dependent on a new chimney being constructed with the word 'STEWARTBY' down one side, together with an interpretation centre to explain the importance of this industry to Bedfordshire. The situation is still unresolved.

Figure 9.3. Peat digging at Flitton Moor, by Thomas Fisher. Peat digging continued in this area of Bedfordshire until the early twentieth century. (The painting is in the care of Flitwick and District Heritage Group, which kindly gave permission for its use in this book.)

Building the machines

The importance of Bedfordshire as an agricultural area stimulated the growth of an agricultural engineering industry, which quickly gained a worldwide reputation, which was regrettably short-lived. While there were always ingenious farmers adapting and tinkering with machinery, the first national figure to emerge from Bedfordshire was John Howard (1791–1878), who opened a business in the High Street, Bedford. His son James Howard became the technical inspiration for advances in engineering and the Howard family brought a new plough to the Great Exhibition in 1851. This model was described by the judge who awarded the prize as *'of small size with a mould board of excellent quality, calculated to give the least resistance in turning the furrow, and much improved'*.

New ploughs and other farming implements were tested at the Clapham Park Estate on the edge of Bedford. The Howard Champion plough became the industry leader and, building on its success, the company embarked on building the Britannia Engineering works in 1856. From the outset, this was planned to

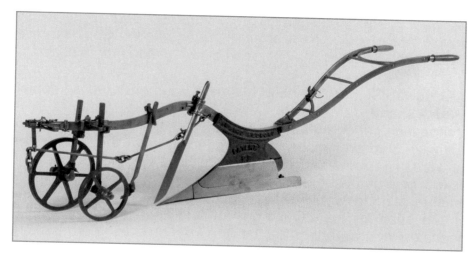

Figure 9.4. The Howard Champion plough. John Howard joined the family firm in 1837, and it was such an important employer in Bedford that it was known simply as 'The Firm'. The business produced a number of very successful ploughs from 1840–50. The Champion plough shown here won numerous prizes in agricultural shows, including a Gold Medal at the Great Exhibition of 1851. The original designer may have been a Mr Armstrong of Wilstead, but it seems likely that the Howard family was also involved in the final design. (Image produced courtesy of The Higgins Bedford. Photograph by Vaughan Dean.)

be a purpose-built factory using advanced production methods. The output from this modern engineering works is best captured by a description from the Victoria County History of 1908, which describes the range of production and the export trade which had been won by the firm of J. and F. Howard:[7]

'The general character of the output may be gathered from the stocks which are stored around the works. Many kinds of plough from the Champion to a light little plough workable by a pony on an allotment; digging ploughs; strong Cape ploughs; Kentish ploughs with a long narrow mould board; an Anglo-American plough in wood and iron; toy-like ploughs for India; ploughs with heavy bent wood beams, as spoken of by Virgil and still in use in Bulgaria and the south of Russia; iron and wood turnwrest[8]

---

[7] The firm went out of business in 1922 and was purchased from the receiver by George Fisher Engineering, which closed in 1993.

[8] A cumbersome, heavy plough popular at the time in Kent.

ploughs; one-way ploughs for South America, Spain and Turkey; double gang, triple and quadruple ploughs; and ploughs for turning six furrows. All these may be seen either finished, or in parts.'

The Howard family had good business acumen, always keeping ahead of the demand for new equipment. In response to a competition set up by the Royal Agricultural Society for a steam cultivator, the firm moved into producing what they called the Howards' Farmers' Engine. The specifics for this competition asked for an implement that would turn over the soil in an efficient manner and that would be an economic substitute for the plough or the spade. The advantages of this new invention quickly became clear, and by 1862 the firm was producing around 200 sets of agricultural engines annually. In 1867, David Greig, in a paper submitted to the British Science Association, described how it worked:

'The steam engine stands on the headland and hauls the implement to and fro by means of a wire rope. All treading and compression of the soil and subsoil associated with horse cultivation is thereby entirely avoided and the implement is driven at a much more rapid pace, throwing up the soil to a greater depth and in a loose state, enabling it to derive full benefit from the influences of the atmosphere. The person who farms by steam has a powerful and untiring force at his disposal, such that he can afford to wait until his land is in an exact state for working.'

Horses could plough around 2 acres of land per day; using steam traction, 8 acres could be ploughed. However, the Bedfordshire market gardens required much smaller, lighter machines that could be operated in compact fields. This became possible with the arrival of the internal combustion engine. Local entrepreneurship led to the development of the first petrol tractor. Dan Albone went from working in a bicycle repair shop in Biggleswade to being an exporter of farm machinery, one of the county's great inventors. His significance is now recognised in Biggleswade by a memorial and picnic area on the bank of the River Ivel close to where he raced his cycles and tested his Ivel machines.

Dan Albone – a man of many parts?

As the age of steam traction in agriculture drew to a close, to be replaced by the internal combustion engine, a Biggleswade inventor, business entrepreneur and racing cyclist turned his attention to the growing need for mechanised field equipment that could be used by the smaller farmer and especially in the market gardening industry of Bedfordshire. Dan Albone, born in Biggleswade in 1860, grew up in a town that was booming, thanks to the arrival of the railway twenty years previously.

The rail connection provided transport for fresh produce to markets in cities, and market gardeners were keen to take advantage of this and expand. Albone's father was a part-time market gardener, but his son saw a gap in a different market and provided a cycle repair service to meet the demand caused by cycling being a fashionable leisure pursuit. He began to work on improving the models of the day.

Dan Albone decided that the best way to advertise his services was to take part in cycle races, and he soon became famous locally. His repair business prospered and expanded to become the Ivel Cycle Company, which produced an interesting mix of models including the Practical Ladies Safety Bicycle and the alarmingly named Hands-Off Safety Bicycle. From pedal cycles it was a short jump to motor-powered bikes, and then in late 1901 came the Ivel Agricultural Motor, driven by an eight horse-power, water-cooled petrol engine, and capable of towing over two tons. Its main advantages, especially in the market garden context, were that it was relatively light compared with a traction engine, compact, yet powerful, and used less fuel, so was cheaper to run.

Local farmers allowed the machine to be trialled on their land and Albone, ever the far-sighted businessman, made sure his prototypes worked in fields that were visible from the railway. The orders flowed in: Albone founded the Ivel Agricultural Motor Company and built a workshop adjacent to the River Ivel, with a bridge from the factory to a demonstration field. The tractor, for that was what it became, won prizes at the Royal Agricultural Show and was taken to agricultural fairs across Britain. Exports to Europe, Australia, New Zealand and Argentina followed. Innovation at the factory continued and in 1906, the Ivel Potato Planter was produced and demonstrated. Sadly, Dan Albone died suddenly in the same year. Later, many skilled staff were called up to serve in the Great War. The company was wound up in 1922.

Bedfordshire as a fruit-growing county

A report on land use in Bedfordshire, part of the 1930 comprehensive land use assessment of Britain, noted that the cold, heavy clays of the county were not favourable for the production of fruit. The author also remarked that where the land was more amenable, it was used for market gardens. However, this overlooks Bedfordshire's earlier, valuable contribution to the national effort to achieve self-sufficiency in food production, especially in the production of apples – and, more importantly, nursery stock for apple growers. As illustrated below, the Laxton family enterprise flourished in Bedford from the 1870s to the 1950s.

Apples and a pear: orchards in Bedfordshire

As mentioned above, during the Second World War a land use survey of Britain was being finalised. Among its detailed observations on crops and livestock in Bedfordshire was a summary on fruit growing which mentioned the Laxton family of plant breeders and their nursery near Bedford. Thomas Laxton (1830–93) was born in Lincolnshire and became a solicitor before his interest in, and talent for, plant breeding prompted a change of career. He quickly achieved commercial success and expanded his business into Bedfordshire, with experimental plots at Kimbolton and at Girtford, near Sandy, followed by an 140-acre plant nursery on Goldington Road, Bedford, which became known locally as 'Laxton's Land'. Over time, the Laxton family produced an amazing number of new varieties of apple, many of which are now English classic varieties, with memorable names such as Lord Lambourne, Laxton's Epicure, Laxton's Fortune, Laxton's Superb and Laxton's Victory. They also produced plums (Laxton's Gage, Early Laxton, Laxton's Supreme), pears, gooseberries, raspberries, currants and strawberries.

After Thomas Laxton's death in 1893, his sons, then his grandsons, carried on the business as the Laxton Brothers, and the family opened a shop in the high street, Bedford, which remained open until 1957. The Goldington Road nursery is now the site of the University of Bedfordshire and schools.

More recently, there has been a reawakening of interest in orchards in the county, and new community orchards are being planted on many sites, such as Park Hill in Bedford. This enterprise is named the Laxton Community orchard, after the pioneering family, and is hidden away behind allotments, adjacent to the Local Nature Reserve at Clapham Park Wood. This site contains 250 fruit trees including many Laxton varieties, as well as a few historic apple varieties, such as Greenup's Pippin and Bess Pool, both of which can be dated to the 1700s, plus heritage varieties imported into Britain including Wyken Pippin from Holland. In 2017, a survey[9] was launched across six counties, including Bedfordshire, to record older orchards and fruit varieties.

The Warden Pear, which is a savoury pear rather than a dessert pear, was sold in London during Shakespeare's lifetime – in fact, he mentioned it *The Winter's Tale*. (For more on this pear, see Margaret Roberts' book, *The Original Warden Pear*.) However, its link to Bedfordshire is tenuous. The Cistercian Abbey at Warden's coat of arms includes three golden pears on a blue background, but this did not appear until the fifteenth century. The abbey, founded in 1135 and dismantled in 1537, has no specific records of pears being grown there. Nevertheless, there were a number of orchards at the abbey site, including a farm or grange known as Orchard Grange.

The growing of damsons (often referred to as 'Aylesbury plums') in Bedfordshire is also well documented. They grow best close to the scarp of the Chilterns Hills, around villages such as Totternhoe, Eaton Bray, Edlesborough, Ivinghoe and Weston Turville. Orchards were established here in the closing years of the nineteenth century and flourished until the 1930s. These orchards cropped erratically but were the foundation of a cottage industry producing pies, puddings and cordials for the local market, especially Luton. The damson skins also yielded a distinctive dye, which was used by the Luton hat industry.

However, all good things must come to an end, and the cycle of agricultural boom–bust continued, with a depression that began in the 1870s and became known as the Great Agricultural Depression. It followed what has been referred to as the Golden Age of British agriculture (the 1840s to 1870). The reasons for the Great Agricultural Depression included a perfect storm of low prices (which slumped as cheap grain from the American prairies and meat from South America carried by faster steam ships undercut local production), a series of poor harvests in the 1870s, and a government policy that favoured the promotion of manufacturing over agriculture. These combined to reduce

---

[9] Funded by the HLF and organised by the University of East Anglia, Orchards East is working with volunteers to survey and record old orchards in the eastern counties of England. See https://www.uea.ac.uk/orchards-east/homefor more information/

the value of land. As succinctly put by Lady Bracknell in *The Importance of Being Earnest* (1895): 'Land has ceased to be either a profit or a pleasure. It gives one a position and prevents one from keeping it up. That is all that can be said for land.'

A series of wet years in the late 1870s led to poor or ruined harvests. By 1886 there were signs of a rural recession, with farms left vacant. Potton seems to have been badly affected, with large numbers of unemployed men, mostly ex-miners of coprolites. In the adjacent county of Huntingdonshire, which was primarily arable, from 1881–85 one farm out of one hundred failed every year. The Great Agricultural Depression saw a reduction of arable land by over 2 million acres, and a corresponding increase in the acreage of permanent pasture.

The government tried to deal with this problem by setting up Royal Commissions in 1882 and 1894, then the Board of Agriculture in 1889. However, by 1914 Britain was importing some 80 per cent of its wheat and almost half of its meat. This was not the best background for a country that was about to become embroiled in the Great War, which caused huge economic and social change across the nation.

CHAPTER 10
RATIONS AND SHORTAGES (1914–55)

The period of depression in British agriculture at the close of the nineteenth century was quickly followed by an upturn, as agriculture was boosted by a worried government that had to work out how to feed the people in wartime. Hunger stalked the combatants in the Great War: men and horses disappeared from the countryside, leaving few fit men to work the land, and shipping routes were disrupted, meaning goods such as fertilisers could not be imported, lowering yields. Agriculture was central to the government's food plans for wartime, and the resultant upheavals led to the break-up of many estates and the introduction of multiple ownership of land.

The Second World War continued, and accelerated, these trends. Horse-drawn implements and large pools of labour were replaced by rapidly improving farm machinery in order to quickly increase productivity, while using less manpower.

By the mid-1950s the rural landscape had changed forever, beginning with the outbreak of the Great War, which brought massive upheaval to the countryside, followed by uncertainty in the interwar years, and then the rationing and food shortages in Britain which continued until the mid-1950s.

Changes during the Great War

Prior to the outbreak of war in 1914, more farmers had turned to pastoral farming, with expectations of a better profit than from cereals. Imports of cheap wheat had reduced the market price for British-grown grain, and the price of wheat in Britain fell by about 50 per cent between the 1870s and the 1890s. Imports from North America had increased thanks to more reliable access to ports and European markets due to the expansion of the rail network (on both sides of the Atlantic). Prices had recovered a little by 1914, but not enough to lead to a change in farmers' cropping patterns.

Figure 10.1a and b. Ampthill plantation forestry felling in 1917: 'The Pines' before and after. Figure 10.1a is from an Ampthill postcard. Figure 10.1b is taken from an official record of the Canadian troops in Bedfordshire (as compiled by Herman Porter and published by the *Bedfordshire Times* and republished by the Ampthill and District Archaeological and Local History Society in 2001). (Many thanks to Stephen Hartley of Ampthill, who supplied both pictures and gave his permission to publish them.)

Cooper's Hill, Ampthill: from rabbit warren to SSSI

Following the introduction of rabbits into Britain, most likely by the Romans, the preparation of specialist warren sites in areas of sandy soil became common. This reached its height in the twelfth century when wardens known as 'warreners' were employed. Rabbits were protected within these areas, and provided meat and fur for landlords. Local records indicate that Ampthill Warren, now known as Cooper's Hill, was used in this way. Woburn Estate plans show this area was known as the Ling Hills – a reference to the heather (or 'ling') covering them.

When the present Ampthill Great Park was a popular area for hunting, animals were driven around from holding areas at the Little Park, adjacent to Cooper's Hill. The hunt was a major leisure activity, with privileged spectators watching the action from specially constructed 'standings' or viewing areas within the park.

The warren was cleared in 1770 and enclosed in the parliamentary enclosure of Ampthill between 1806 and 1808. The 7th Duke of Bedford then planted Scots pine shortly afterwards, which led to the confusing local name for the area: it is still known as the Firs, as is the adjacent local school. At this time, local people would probably have lost access to this area for the collection of fuel wood and furze. This coniferous planting was ecologically sound, as pines thrived in the marginal sandy soils and the short, steep slopes in this area of the Greensand Ridge made any other form of cultivation difficult.

The next radical change in land use came during the Great War, with the wholesale felling of pine trees to meet the demand for timber at the front in France and at home in Britain. The 106 Canadian Corps arrived in Ampthill in August 1917 and was soon joined by 100 more men, draught horses and equipment specially imported from Canada. The speed of the felling was impressive, with 110 trees felled on the first day of work. The operation grew with the addition of Portuguese labourers, a saw mill to deal with the felled trees, and a light railway to transport the wood. The operation was later expanded to include additional camps at Maulden, Millbrook and Flitwick.

The Firs, or Cooper's Hill, is now owned by Ampthill Town Council and is a popular and valued walk for residents. Ecological management of the site is encouraging the return of the lowland heath vegetation, a declining habitat across southern England. In an attempt to conserve this heathland, the site has been demarcated as an SSSI. However, the challenge of protecting a very popular location, close to a town with a growing population, and with vegetation that is a fire risk, should not be underestimated.

However, by 1917 the submarine offensive in the north Atlantic concentrated British minds and the government set about increasing the supply of home-grown potatoes and cereals. There are records of estates such as Potsgrove breaking up parkland to grow arable crops. Heavy steam ploughs were sometimes used to bring land into production: the John Allen Company of Bedford was engaged in the manufacture of heavy steam equipment, and sold steam ploughs to the government. This was not always a success, as heavy machinery on heavy land after a wet spring led to quagmires of mud in many places.

Perhaps the most striking change in Bedfordshire land use was the felling of plantations which gave character to areas such as the Greensand Ridge. The nineteenth-century forests that had been planted by large landlords, especially the Dukes of Bedford, were felled for much-needed timber in both England and the trenches in France. Estates were forced to plough up grassland, and many of the great houses were requisitioned for military use or fell into disrepair. At Cooper's Hill, by Ampthill, the felling of a plantation known as 'The Pines' in 1917 marked a further change in the long history of the heathland site.

The interwar years

At the end of hostilities in 1918, agriculture returned to economically difficult conditions, with people continuing to drift to towns and cities. By 1939, less than 20 per cent of people lived rurally. While a few farmers overcame these challenges, many farms returned to grazing. This became known as 'dog and stick farming' – these were the only tools needed to work a farm. Wages in agriculture were poor, farm workers' relationships with their employers soured, the stock of rural housing was antiquated or worse, and the countryside was plagued by a scourge of rabbits. No wonder there was little private investment. Farmers in north Bedfordshire tell tales of cart-loads of rabbits being either sold or disposed of. In some cases selling the rabbits almost met the cost of rent, but crops suffered accordingly. The low points of this farming depression were 1922–25 and 1929–30. The derelict state of some land was captured by the writer Henry Williamson[10] in his description of a Norfolk farm taken over in the 1930s: 'The farm

---

[10] Henry Williamson was a well-known agricultural and nature writer in the interwar years and during the Second World War. His best known books are *Tarka the Otter* and *The Story of a Norfolk Farm*.

was weedy, hedges tall and ragged, gates broken or fallen, the roads were bogs or deep ruts, the buildings ruinous and rat-ridden, the meadows were snipe bogs, the wood full of broken trees, and dead elderberry.'

This rural malaise took place against a background of national economic difficulties. One government initiative to counter the economic ills was to encourage resettlement schemes, which offered unemployed men, mostly miners, the opportunity to become smallholder farmers. In Bedfordshire such schemes were launched at Wyboston and Potton. the Land Settlement Association initiative history in Bedfordshire is summarised below.

The Land Settlement Association: the entry point to farming

Within earshot of the traffic on the busy A1, there still exists an interesting fragment of Bedfordshire rural history. Beside a minor road close to Chawston are a number of smallholdings, which originated as plots of land owned by the Land Settlement Association (LSA). Most of these holdings have been built on, and are now attractive private houses surrounded by valuable plots of land (the original plots were 5 acres). The idea was to provide a new start for unemployed men and their families, who would work in a co-operative on a centralised estate. During the early 1930s, many redundant miners from the north-east of England and Kent took up this offer. This model was also trialled at Potton, where there were around thirty holdings. The incomers were given a house, and were expected to work on what was quaintly described as 'a three-legged stool' of production: pigs, poultry and horticulture. All the produce was marketed collectively and sold only through the LSA. The experiment was partly successful, but the records show 'a constant churn of people' trying to make the system work. In 1939 the plots were used as part of the war effort, and men with agricultural experience were engaged to work on them. After the war these became statutory smallholdings managed by Bedfordshire County Council, and seen as 'the first rung on the farming ladder'.

The evidence of previous land use can still be seen in the abandoned greenhouses and the uniform style of outbuildings close to the A1. In some cases, the modern use of the land reflects the government's brave attempt to provide employment in the agricultural sector. While some plots have become boarding kennels or paddocks for horses, there are modern, state-of-the-art greenhouses which still connect this area to its former land use.

On the positive side of the balance sheet, this period most likely saw the largest change in land ownership since the dissolution of the monasteries, with more farms coming on to the market and more new tenancy agreements on offer, allowing new energy to enter the farming industry. The government also acted on the need to increase food security, and in 1931 made a determined effort to better understand what the country could produce. The government came up with the idea of carrying out a national survey of all parishes in the country, with the help of an astonishing 200,000 volunteers. The resulting record of land use is akin to the detail provided 800 years previously in the Domesday Book. The idea of such a survey eventually won support, but some of the major landowners in Bedfordshire required persuasion to take part. Under the supervision of the Director of Education, the work was completed by August 1931. The report, which was published a decade later, during the Second World War, gives a glimpse into rural Bedfordshire, along with sketch maps and notes on villages in the county.

The interwar years also saw a growing public enthusiasm for the countryside, and the foundation of the Federation of Ramblers (which later became the Ramblers' Association and is now known as the Ramblers). At the same time, public concerns over the loss of valued and loved areas of countryside led to the founding of the Council for the Preservation of Rural England (CPRE) in 1926 (now the Campaign to Protect Rural England). The land use survey therefore took place at a time when the countryside was changing from a way of life to a means of production.

The Second World War: ploughing-up campaigns

The beginning of the Second World War in 1939 returned the national issue of food security to the forefront of public – and government – concerns. County War Agricultural Executive Committees were formed with the aim of increasing domestic food production. They had the power to impose quotas on land ploughed, and offered incentives of £2 per acre for converting to arable farming. These committees also arranged for the distribution of tractors. However, it soon became clear that while the government had a good grasp of the potential of the land, it had much less understanding of the farmers who worked the land. This led to the controversial National Farm Survey (1941–43),

Counting the crops: the 1931 land use survey of Britain

In 1941, a substantial volume of information on the land and crops throughout Britain was published, thanks to a remarkable public effort to record land use, field by field, across the country. It was completed under the direction of a senior academic, Professor Dudley Stamp. Maps of Bedfordshire began to be published in 1934 (Luton), and the final sheet (Bedford) followed in 1937. At a scale of 6 inches to 1 mile, these were based on old Ordnance Survey sheets dating as far back as 1907. These elderly topographic maps were judged to be adequate for the task, and the Bedfordshire report noted that there were few changes from the 1907 mapping to field boundaries and urban development areas. The Bedfordshire report (compiled by C.E. Fitchett) to accompany these maps was not published until 1943 and is Part 55 in the national survey, titled *The Land of Britain*. Fitchett makes many interesting observations in his introduction, such as describing Bedfordshire as a 'thoroughfare county', and concludes: 'Bedfordshire is one of the lesser known English counties. It has at first sight no obvious claim to distinction.'

Fitchett's report is a wonderful snapshot of land use in the early 1930s. At the time, over 80 per cent of Bedfordshire was in either crops or grass, which was higher than in most surrounding counties. Fitchett noted the complex pattern of soil conditions across the landscape, and the report includes numerous sketch maps of parishes showing the cropping patterns.

which took the unprecedented step of grading farmers according to their management skills. Farmers' performance was graded A, B or C. Those in the latter class were judged to have 'personal failings', and could have a tenancy ended. These severe regulations led to a few suicides and many fights with bureaucrats.

In north Bedfordshire, as in other parts of England, farmers struggled to grow unsuitable crops in unfavourable soils. Potatoes and flax grown under the county quota system were especially unpopular, as a number of wet summers made harvesting a muddy experience with clogged machinery. Many country houses were requisitioned for military use (such as Ampthill and Chicksands), while swathes of parkland were ploughed up in the drive to 'dig for victory'. The Women's Land Army was on the move, bringing new ideas which challenged the more relaxed view of estate management as seen by many larger landowners. Gardens of great houses such as Wrest Park were either turned over to vegetable production, or kept going with much reduced labour. Some were simply abandoned. The lawns at Woburn were early victims of the plough, being turned over in 1939.

Following the war, the parklands in Bedfordshire continued this wartime trend towards being converted to arable production, with intensive farming practices leading to the loss of parkland features, notably in-field trees, which hindered modern methods of cultivation. These changes to the character of the parklands in the county were to become symbolic of the ongoing tension which today pitches production and the economical use of land against protection and conservation. In Bedfordshire the debate is as lively as it is elsewhere in England, and the recent impacts of land use change are very evident. There have been losses to countryside quality, such as the removal of hedge lines, as well as some notable gains, such as the rehabilitation of former quarry sites and the importance now placed on conserving lowland heath and protecting ancient woodland.

The new users of the countryside

The incoming Attlee government of 1945 brought in sweeping changes and had a new energy and vision after the long years of war. A determined effort was made to improve the quality of rural life, including the acceleration of electrification programmes to bring power to rural settlements and farms. The Agriculture Act 1947 introduced a level of security for farm tenants and an Agricultural Wages Board was introduced at this time. The post-war government's agricultural policies were both bold and interventionist: the government provided subsidies for land improvement (for example, the removal of bracken and the widespread application of lime to farmland). As a result, farm output across Britain increased by 20 per cent between 1947 and 1952. However, there was a price to pay for this agricultural expansion. Around 40 per cent of all England's ancient woodland has been uprooted since 1945, and the motorway building and road improvement programmes in the 1960s and since have continued to fragment or remove older woods. The cost of removing a mature oak was often as low as sixpence.

The importance of agriculture was a cornerstone of the great social changes introduced by the Atlee government, with the ultimate aim of bringing an end to rationing. By 1951, when the government was defeated in the general election, determined efforts had already been made to modernise the rural economy. Farmers' appetite for improved and modern agricultural machinery had been stimulated by the wartime importation of US-built tractors, and this was recognised in the establishment of the National Institute of Agricultural Engineering at a new site at Wrest Park, Silsoe in 1947. This was followed by the opening in 1962 of the National College of Agricultural Engineering, which over the next few decades forged a considerable reputation internationally as a premier education facility.

The mass trespass of Kinder Scout in the Peak District has become a landmark event. It took place on 24 April 1932 to protest against the fact that walkers in England and Wales were denied access to areas of open country. It sparked off a social movement in which the swelling urban population began to demand the right to spend time outdoors in areas that had previously been private. In response, Atlee's government began to recognise and classify a network of sites judged to have scientific value, ranging from chalk grassland to ancient monuments. All these conservation areas have been stoutly defended by the public ever since, and are now accepted as giving a special character to the countryside. One of the longest lasting measures has been the National Parks and Access to the Countryside Act 1949, which made possible the present system of designated sites, with the National Parks as the flagship sites. The first National Park was the Peak District, created in 1952. Most importantly, public footpaths became formalised in the recognition of 'rights of way', included in the 1949 Act. This meant that the public had legal access to footpaths and also the 'right to roam' in certain upland areas.

The legacy in Bedfordshire is a network of paths that are well used by a wide variety of people, from ramblers to dog walkers. Later these paths were linked to create long-distance trails such as the Greensand Ridge Walk and the Bunyan Trail. Bridleways were also recognised, and the recent popularity of off-road cycling and mountain biking depends on the legal right to use these cross-country routes.

Social change also meant that people had more time for leisure. The growing urban population looked to the countryside for recreation and fulfilment. The countryside was no longer seen simply as a place to produce food; now there was an expectation that the outdoors should be accessible and attractive to a variety of users. Governments since 1960 have struggled to keep the farming industry competitive in a global food market, and also to meet the rising expectations of an urban population for access.

Finding a balance between the two would be the next challenge.

CHAPTER 11
FINDING A BALANCE – PUBLIC FOOTPATHS AND PUBLIC INTEREST (1955–2016)

'Urban planning makes a positive difference to people's lives and helps to deliver homes, jobs and better opportunities for all – while protecting and enhancing the natural and historic environment, and conserving the countryside and open spaces for everyone and for the future.'

The 1985 Government Planning Directive

The end of the Second World War in Europe in 1945 did not immediately see the end of rationing in the UK, which prevailed until the mid-1950s. Eventually the nation was freed to take a more relaxed view of food production, and this stability provides a starting point to trace the changes in rural land use up to the UK's decision to leave the European Union in 2016. At the time of writing, there is only informed speculation on the agricultural support arrangements which will follow Brexit in the next decade.

In Bedfordshire from the mid-1950s onwards, the changes were significant. Perhaps the most noteworthy trend has been a steady growth in public awareness of the issue of countryside access. This had led to the legal protection of public footpaths and conservation areas being designated, or recognised, as worthy of protection. There is also a growing awareness that even a small area, such as a local nature reserve, can be a special place with its own character, and is worth fighting for.

Today there is also an increased awareness of the health benefits of outdoor pursuits, specifically walking. This has engaged more people in the countryside, along with an increase in volunteering by individuals, which has helped to conserve landscapes and historic gardens. These trends have been accompanied by a renewed interest in food production, which has impacted on farming practice. Additionally, the issue of food miles and the volume of food now imported into the UK has reopened previous historical debates over food security. All of these factors may lead to significant changes in agriculture.

An important development in Bedfordshire has been the regeneration of the Marston Vale area with a forty-year plan to enhance the damaged landscape following the closure of the last brickworks in 2008. The remaining four chimneys are now Grade II listed. At the height of brick production, there were 162 chimneys in the Vale (see Figure 9.2), but today the landscape is being transformed from the dereliction which followed industrialisation. The picture below dates from the 1990s.

Figure 11.1. Marston Vale landfill site in the 1990s. This shows the site at Brogborough, now within the Forest of Marston Vale, when Bedfordshire was seen as the landfill site for London rubbish. Trains from the capital conveyed non-sorted material to the older brick clay excavations. (Produced by courtesy of the Forest of Marston Vale Image Library.)

What is in the public interest?

The idea of public interest is most often applied in the legal world, but now has a much wider application and was recognised after the war, specifically with the National Parks and Access to the Countryside Act 1949. This Act provided the framework for the creation of National Parks and Areas of Outstanding Natural Beauty (AONB) in England and Wales, and also addressed public rights of way and access to open land. At the top of the hierarchy are National Parks, with high levels of protection from developments that are perceived to be damaging to the landscape, scenery or wildlife. The Act gave local government the power to define nature reserves, make provision for the protection and upkeep of public footpaths, and secure access to the countryside. This was strengthened by the Wildlife and Countryside Act 1981, which defined protected species and has since been amended.

In Bedfordshire, there are three National Nature Reserves: King's Wood within Rushmere County Park (63 hectares); Knocking Hoe on the chalk downs (7 hectares); and Barton Hills (44 hectares). Below National Nature Reserves in hierarchy of protection are Local Nature Reserves, of which Bedfordshire has twenty, including Flitwick Wood and Fenlake Meadows. These are defined as places of special local wildlife or geological interest. There are also Local Geological Sites, which are given the same status and are monitored by the Bedfordshire Geology Group.

One of the strongest levels of protection is reserved for Sites of Special Scientific Interest (SSSIs), which – as the name suggests – are important for the recording and monitoring of flora and fauna, and changing environmental conditions. The Flitwick Moor SSSI is a good example: monitoring of water flowing into the reserve can be used to estimate the changing acidity levels and how these influence the vegetation. The reserve was created to conserve plants that flourish in an environment where the groundwater is slightly acid. However, this delicate balance can be skewed by falling groundwater levels in the Greensand rock, which are replaced by more alkaline water flowing from the chalk.

In addition, local government has the power to recognise County Wildlife Sites, which are localities with significant nature conservation value but outside the statutory protected areas. In Bedfordshire these may be as small as a churchyard (such as at Everton or a few hectares of calcareous meadows at Totternhoe). Some 7 per cent of Bedfordshire is designated as County Wildlife Sites – there are over 400 sites. These may only be fragments of the countryside, but they often bridge the gap between the urban and rural and provide small havens for wildlife.

Before the idea of the landscape in itself being important and worth cherishing could be embedded, the hangover from food shortages during the war years had to recede into history. During the 1950s and 1960s a generation that had experienced war and rationing was more concerned with growing food: self-sufficiency was central to the national agenda. Farming modernisation and productivity was therefore paramount, and the exciting glimpses of modern machinery provided by American imports during the war paved the way for new technology to help feed the nation. The experience of the wartime farmers instructed to plough up land was still alive and influenced the notion of a self-sufficient nation: this was reflected in the 1947 Agriculture Act, which emphasised increased yields. Ancient woodland was removed to 'restore' land to agriculture. There was a real national pride in productivity, pushing other interests such as countryside protection or conservation onto the back burner. The government's decision to expand the National Institute of Agricultural Engineering and move to a new extensive experimental estate at Wrest Park at Silsoe in 1947 was in response to public concern. The site was carefully chosen to straddle the light, easily worked soils on the edge of the Greensand geology and the less favourable, tenacious heavy clay soil.

Preservation and protection

As mentioned earlier, the poet John Clare mourned the loss of common land during enclosure, and the accompanying loss of access to large areas of countryside. He was in many ways tapping into a deep folk memory which is still alive today. The feeling that the public has a traditional right to roam the countryside, despite the clear legal definition of 'private property', underlies many planning disputes. There is a strongly held view that the countryside belongs to the nation, not to the few individuals or institutions that may be in temporary possession of the land. The *Council for the Preservation of Rural England* (CPRE) was founded to advance the arguments for protection, while an equally vocal lobby was concerned about the danger of public access.

As car ownership increased and more people wanted to spend their leisure time in the countryside, the government moved, albeit slowly, to catch up. As far back as 1966 the title of a government report, 'Leisure in the Countryside', accurately captured the competition between farming and public access. During the 1980s and 1990s the commitment of both national and local government to countryside concerns was at an all-time high. At the national level, the government promised twelve new community forests across England, including the Forest of Marston Vale in Bedfordshire, which was enthusiastically supported by local government.

The Forest of Marston Vale: land restoration projects

The impressive transformation of the landscapes within Marston Vale is thanks to the concept of community forests, which came from The Netherlands during the 1930s. In 1934 an ambitious forestation scheme was begun close to the rapidly expanding urban area around Amsterdam, mainly to provide employment in a time of agricultural depression. In the 1990s, this idea reached the UK.

With the closure of the brick-making industry of Marston Vale, the area was ripe for investment and in 1991 it was selected to be one of twelve new community forests in England. The area, scarred by the brick-making industry, was seen as a blight on the landscape.

The challenge was to use trees to repair and soften the damaged landscape, and at the same time revitalise the communities around the forest. The government's target is to plant six million trees by 2031. Within the forest area is the Millennium Country Park (225 hectares) which has a Forest Centre that is used for a variety of community, educational, social and business gatherings. The presence of the National Forest will introduce a wooded landscape along the improved A421 road corridor south of Bedford.

During the 1980s the former Bedfordshire County Council had a keen interest in public engagement. It published maps of Bedfordshire's geology which are still used today by teachers, and one initiative by the Council was the publication of a slim booklet entitled *Champion Trees of Bedfordshire* (1993). This useful publication listed all the important individual trees that are part of the landscape in the county.

Many people are familiar with Tree Preservation Orders, which are administered by local government and are a requirement before felling or lopping significant trees in residential areas. There are, however, other tree classifications which identify trees of special significance in the landscape and offer enhanced levels of protection.

Woodman, spare that tree: champion, heritage and veteran trees

The 1993 publication which listed outstanding individual tees in Bedfordshire defined a 'champion tree' by size alone. Within the county the surveyors located 219 specimens, which were then recorded. These trees were either the tallest, the largest (defined by the girth of the trunk 1.3 metres (4.2 feet) above the ground), or rare in some other way. The authors note that, at the time of surveying, only 6 per cent of the county was woodland, making Bedfordshire one of the least wooded areas of England. Some 85 per cent of Bedfordshire's woods are privately owned. However, the scarcity of woodland was compensated for by the wealth of species that have found sanctuary in the county's widespread parklands. Notable in this record are trees which were ranked as British champions, such as the golden oak at Luton Hoo. An interesting map in the booklet shows the woodland areas surveyed, which range from Swineshead Wood in the north of the county to Luton Hoo in the south. There is a marked concentration of important tree collections in the parklands along the Greensand Ridge. Listed in the top twenty largest trees are many oaks at Woburn Park, the giant redwoods at Wrest Park and, less common, a turkey oak at Ickwell Bury.

A further categorisation is that of 'veteran trees' – this takes note of a tree's age and cultural value, not just its size. This alternative classification of trees in the countryside reflects the historic role of individual species. There is no precise definition of a veteran tree, but there is a third classification: 'heritage trees'. The definition here is a tree with unique value that is considered to be irreplaceable. In Bedfordshire the John Bunyan tree at Harlington (where the iterant preacher was arrested before being sent to Bedford Gaol) would qualify. Another example is the Beaumont tree (close to the Silsoe–Flitton crossroads, which marked the site where a highwayman was executed in 1751). The tree later became the site where local people performed rites in the hope of warding off an ague or fever, similar to malaria, which was prevalent in the wetlands of Flitton Moor.

Since 1988 the charity the National Tree Register has been compiling a unique record of notable and ancient trees in Britain. The database, which now includes around 270,000 trees, is maintained by volunteers.

The new public interest

The title of this chapter, 'Finding a Balance', indicates how changes in land use and farming have impacted one area of England. What is unmistakable is the change in mindset in regard to how we view the countryside. There has been a real increase in public interest in how the countryside functions, and especially in how our food is produced. Cases of bovine spongiform encephalopathy (BSE), commonly known as mad cow disease; the shock of the outbreak of foot and mouth disease, which effectively closed the countryside; scandals over the fraudulent labelling of food; and widespread concern over the dominance of large supermarkets in the food chain has led to people taking an increasingly active interest in British farming. The recent rise in organic production and small-scale artisanal producers, the popularity of vegetable boxes, and recent television programmes on farming are all evidence of a public-led demand for not only better food but also a greater understanding of how food is produced. These changes have forced the farming industry and major supermarkets to respond. One noticeable change has been farmers' move from a protectionist view (summed up by 'Get off my land') to a more measured public welcome on Open Farm Sundays, for example. This increased public interest is likely to intensify as the UK withdraws from the European Union, and EU payments to the UK stop.

Making space for nature

The countryside, especially in Bedfordshire, is shaped by a conglomeration of small and sometimes large businesses, ranging from smallholders with a few paddocks and a livery yard to a number of substantial farming businesses with many hectares of land across neighbouring counties. All operate within a planning framework set by the government, and all strive to make a profit. Within this, nature conservation, open accessible space, and outdoor leisure need to find a few hectares for public use and / or protection. In 2010, a government report by a respected academic (Lawton, 2010) bravely attempted to chart a way forward. In a review of England's wildlife sites, John Lawton recognised three important aspects of conservation: (1) we needed more land under some form of protection; (2) existing nature reserves were fragmented and limited by the lack of connecting 'nature corridors';

and (3) some of the existing protected areas were not thriving, but were being degraded. Remember that Bedfordshire has about 6% of woodland cover compared to 13% for the UK overall.

Since the Lawton Report, a raft of initiatives have begun to take root. These are now making an impact. A Nature Improvement Area has been defined along the Greensand Ridge. This is, as the title suggests, an area of conservation significance where there is deemed to be a need for marked improvement. In Bedfordshire, the Greensand Trust, the Wildlife Trust for Bedfordshire, Cambridgeshire and Northamptonshire and the Royal Society for the Protection of Birds (RSPB) have joined Central Bedfordshire Council and Natural England to improve conservation areas across this important and well-used belt of countryside. These agencies are committed to working together and with others to achieve a real, lasting difference to the habitats, species and landscape along the Greensand Ridge by strengthening ecological networks, enhancing existing sites, and linking these together across the wider countryside.

More recently, the Bedfordshire Local Nature Partnership (BLNP) has taken the approach of involving business and the countryside. The BLNP has embarked on a project which attempts to assess the value of natural assets through the emerging economic techniques of natural capital accounting. The aim is to encourage an appreciation of the natural resources in the county by attempting an audit of the countryside's value to society overall. The BLNP points out the cost of mental health to the taxpayer in Bedfordshire is currently more than £500 million per year, and that being out of doors and actively engaging with nature has been proven to be beneficial for health, both mental and physical.

Walking and well-being

Current government advice is that everyone should walk for at least 30 minutes per day. Walking now ranks as the most popular outdoor pursuit. Bedfordshire has a number of ramblers groups, some of which meet four or five days each week. The Bedfordshire Walking Festival (www.bedswalkfest.co.uk/) continues to grow in popularity, and there has been encouragement for those not familiar with the countryside to have a taste of walking in a group with an experienced leader. Some churches have joined the walking movement, and many Bedfordshire villages now publish newsletters or have websites which include short strolls or longer walks centred on a village or local pub. This interest has been complemented by initiatives to make a walk more interesting, with sculptures being added to Rushmere Country Park, Chicksands Wood and Flitwick Manor Park.

The irony of this upsurge in interest is that all these walks rely on the network of public footpaths, the maintenance of which is the responsibility of local government, which has been forced to react to funding cuts by reducing staff. Previously, the council had dedicated footpath officers who could investigate issues and respond to reports of footpath damage; now, this job is being combined with other functions, or even removed. The importance of walking as a leisure pursuit can be seen in the diagram below which was generated during preparation work for the Greensand Country Landscape Partnership initiative.

Figure 11.2. This figure shows the responses received from a general audience when they were asked what countryside activity they enjoyed most. Walking in the countryside was the most valued activity. (Reproduced with permission of the Greensand Country Landscape Partnership.)

If many people are interested in being out of doors and walking in the countryside, how can this be channelled into a better understanding of landscape topics? Many walking groups seem to simply want to get from A to B, to reach their lunchtime pub destination with little time to stand and stare at the landscape through which they are passing. Some small headway has been made with expert groups reaching out to promote educational engagement in areas such as geology. The Bedfordshire Geology Group has promoted geo-trails in Bedfordshire at Clophill and in the Jurassic limestone around Bromham. However, there is likely to be a greater demand in future for similar types of interaction. How about farm walks, which allow people to understand more about modern agriculture, or knowledgeable excursions to show off some of Bedfordshire's varied woodlands, both ancient and modern? As we move after 2022 into a new era of public funding, this informed interested public will be an asset. There will be decisions to be made on what to fund – on what is considered to be in the public interest. In the debate, there will be arguments on the value of land – not the cost per acre, but how much we care about making space for nature, and what we feel it is important to protect.

Volunteering to make it happen

A short walk from the main street of Clophill village is the site of St Mary's Old Church. Many residents of Bedfordshire will recall with horror newspaper stories of black arts and alternative worship apparently practised there, which plagued the site for a decade or more. Now the crumbling tower of the church has been stabilised and a safe platform constructed to give people a view of the surrounding Greensand Ridge; there are beautifully designed public information boards to explain the landscape and history; and next door there is a wonderful purpose-built eco-centre facility that is used by groups ranging from ramblers resting their feet after a day walking the Ridge to local school groups learning about wildflowers. Plans are under way for a geology wall to demonstrate the variety of the local rocks. This initiative is the work of a small body of dedicated volunteers who raised the money to transform a derelict site into a community resource. Converting the former sand extraction pit into Tiddenfoot Nature Reserve, close to Leighton Buzzard, is another example of a Bedfordshire volunteer-supported initiative.

These examples represent a growing trend in volunteering. This movement has tapped into countryside issues. Village partnerships to promote and look after footpaths are essentially community based, and many people volunteer to help with gardening and landscaping with English Heritage, the Marston Vale Country Park and the Bedfordshire Rural Communities Charity – without them, these valued landscape sites could not operate. English Heritage's plans at Wrest Park using community groups and schools are particularly ambitious. Its vision is to recreate the landscape of the Old Park area, adjacent to the present gardens, by planting trees in the style of a late-nineteenth-century parkland. It has begun by focusing on three large blocks of land. This requires the planting of trees, using a first-edition Ordnance Survey map as a guide to the design. The challenge of planting the planned 22,000 trees would be impossible to envisage without volunteer help.

Professionals engaged in the conservation business will admit that, without the army of volunteers, it would be impossible to keep valued and historically interesting places open to the public. Volunteering takes many forms: for example, community orchards across Bedfordshire (at Park Road and at the Guru Nanak Gurdwara temple in Bedford), as well as at Southill, Great Billington, Mowsbury, Blow's Downs and Riseley, are providing opportunities for local people to learn new skills and volunteer their help, as well as protecting valuable wildlife areas. In 2018 a new initiative to record and map orchards – both old and new – in the county began, again using volunteers. Volunteering can also act as a stepping stone into full-time careers, and practical training in the rural industries is offered by educational institutions such as Shuttleworth College close to Shefford.

While future governments may rediscover the need to take account of the Public Interest – in the formal sense of the welfare or well-being of the public – in making investment decisions and funding policies, without an underpinning 'public interest', expressed though community participation and active involvement or individual volunteering, new initiatives will flounder or be marginalised.

However, there is also the danger that, in focusing on the tangible and direct impacts, we overlook the less immediate reasons for making sure we look after the countryside. The importance of the landscape to poets and painters, and the human need to interact with nature, are being increasingly recognised as the population becomes more urban and less connected to the land. Chapter 12 discusses several important historical personalities who have drawn inspiration from Bedfordshire's landscape.

CHAPTER 12
PREACHERS, PAINTERS AND POETS

'As I walked through the wilderness of the world, I lighted on a certain place where there was a den, and I laid me down in that place to sleep. And as I sleep I dreamed a dream.'

The opening lines of *The Pilgrim's Progress* by John Bunyan (1678)

The preacher

It would be difficult to write anything about Bedfordshire without a reference to John Bunyan (1628–88). In fact, *The Pilgrim's Progress*[11] is not only a powerful literary and religious text; it also celebrates the countryside and landscape through which Bunyan walked, preached, and carried out his trade. The author was a passionate and eloquent preacher and a writer with a vivid imagination, but he also clearly had the ability to capture the essence of the countryside he knew so well. Bunyan created memorable phrases to describe the topography, such as the 'slough of despond' and the 'celestial mountains', and these imprinted many of the features of Bedfordshire's landscape onto the public imagination. We also have to assume that Bunyan was a useful tinker, a valued craftsman and a welcome visitor to rural households.

The connection to the land is the basis for several books which have Bunyan and his countryside as the central theme. *The Bunyan Country* by Charles Hooper has the subtitle *Landmarks of the Pilgrim's Progress*. Published in 1928, this handsome text is illustrated by charming black-and-white line drawings of the local landscape. The author identified the 'slough of despond' as an area of heavy clay land along the A5 near Tilsworth. An earlier book by Albert John Foster (1901) attempted to identify exact locations in *The Pilgrim's Progress*. In *Bunyan Country: Studies*

---

[11] First published in 1678 with the full title *The Pilgrim's Progress from This World to That Which is to Come*, the book has been translated into around 200 languages and has never been out of print. Bunyan began to write it when he was held in Bedford Goal on the charge of preaching while not an ordained Church of England minister.

in the Bedfordshire Topography of the Pilgrim's Progress, Foster places the 'slough of despond' between Elstow and the Greensand Ridge.

Passing over the debatable point of local geographical interpretation, the real point of interest is that Bunyan's journeys in the mid-seventeenth century still seem relevant and interesting today. While the 'slough of despond' has long since been drained and is now productive wheat land, the flat and largely featureless landscape of the clays is still an essential part of the Bedfordshire countryside.

A little hill called Lucre: the mine at Pulloxhill

While John Bunyan was imprisoned at Bedford, he allowed himself to think about his life, spent roaming the countryside of Bedfordshire. The topography and character of the county therefore play a central role in his book, *The Pilgrim's Progress*, which has been described as an immortal allegory charting the journey of the hero, Christian, across a landscape filled with moral and physical hazards. One intriguing example is when Christian encounters the keeper of a silver mine at Pulloxhill. Bunyan ensures his hero is not tempted by easy riches and 'turned aside', but his companions chose to enter the mine – and were never seen again.

There are historical records of an unsuccessful gold mining operation at a site in the vicinity of the village, and there is today a field called Gold Close. This mine was opened in 1680 and would have been known to Bunyan in his travels. Until recently, the field bore the scars of old mining pits, now water-filled. The gold rush ended when people realised that the 'gold' was in fact flakes of mica from weathering rock. One mystery remains – why did Bunyan describe it as a silver mine in his book, rather than a gold mine?

The painters

The influence of Bunyan is so strong that Edward Callam (1904–80), from Elstow, set out to create a suite of paintings based on scenes from *The Pilgrim's Progress*. His work, which is now in the National Art Collection and held in trust by Luton Culture, is a powerful representation of the Bedfordshire landscape – sometimes as seen today, and sometimes as imagined at the time of Bunyan. This little-known group of paintings is referred to as the Celestial County series. Examples include Callam's evocative

The Slough of Despond, which is of a wetland area close to Elstow. Marsh or bog such as this would have been common when Bunyan was alive. Another is a view of what the artist called *The Valley of the Shadow.* It was painted in the mid-twentieth century as the view from above Millbrook village. Since he painted it, this landscape has already altered significantly.

Figure 12.1. *The Slough of Despond* by Edward Callam. The painting shows Cardington Brook in winter, flooding the fields adjacent to the painter's cottage close to Elstow Village. The accompanying quotation from *The Pilgrim's Progress* reads: 'They drew near to a very miry slough that was in the midst of the plain, and they being heedless did both fall suddenly into the bog. The name of the slough was Despond.' (The painting is held by Luton Culture and is part of the collection at Wardown Museum. Reproduced here with kind permission of Luton Culture.)

The painter Thomas Fisher (1772–1836) also chose to focus on local country scenes. Perhaps his most interesting painting is *Flitton Moor* (Figure 9.3), in which peat diggers are seen stacking cut turf. The painting is a useful reminder of a past landscape, now largely drained, as well as a reminder of a long-gone way of life. However, the former peat diggings are still visible at the Duck End nature reserve at Maulden and at Flitwick Moor, now an important botanical SSSI. Fisher's other paintings mostly depict village or town scenes, including a watercolour of Houghton House at Ampthill and the market cross at Leighton Buzzard.

Throughout history, artists' work has reflected the fashions and trends of the time. Three works by the famous painter of horses, George Stubbs, provide an insight into the way in which the improving landlords of the eighteenth century viewed their property and land. Commissioned by Lord Torrington, then owner of the Southill Estate, Stubbs painted these pictures in 1767, featuring workers on the estate. The best known is entitled *Lord Torrington's Hunt Servants Setting Out from Southill, Bedfordshire*, and – as you might expect – it shows lots of horses and dogs as well as huntsmen and retainers. Another is entitled *Lord Torrington's Steward and Gamekeeper, with Dogs*. It portrays a mounted steward followed on foot by a gun-carrying gamekeeper, accompanied by dogs, as they pass through a woodland. The purpose of this painting could either be to exhibit the wealth of the landowner (shown by the well-managed woodland and the impressive steward on horseback), or to make it clear that visitors are not welcome in the woods, and that the woods are patrolled by dogs and a man with a gun. (These paintings can be viewed today at Upton House, Warwickshire, a National Trust property.)

The fashion among the landed elite for commissioning art to mark the success of their progressive agricultural endeavours was followed by the 4th Duke of Bedford in a work by George Garrard (1760–1826) entitled *Woburn Sheepshearing*. Garrard's large painting, dated 1804, captures the busy scene at this agricultural fair. The duke, mounted, is surrounded by dozens of other notables admiring his improved breeds of livestock.

In the nineteenth century, Arthur Anderson (1861–1904) painted watercolours of landscapes around Bedford, including a fine winter scene at Fenlake Meadows on the Great Ouse. Remarkably, he had five brothers, also all competent artists. A more recent artist has captured the nature reserve at Flitwick Moor. This painting has been used on the title page of this book. Jim Trolinger, a contemporary painter, now based in the USA, painted this wet woodland a number of times.

The poets

Edward Thomas (1878–1917)

'Much has been written of travel, far less of the road.' (Edward Thomas, *The Icknield Way*, 1913)

Great War poet Edward Thomas traced the route of the Icknield Way in the spring of 1911, while in the depths of one of his worst bouts of depression. The resulting book, *The Icknield Way*, was published in 1913. His work was dominated by the countryside: his journey on foot, or sometimes by cycle, began in Thetford, Norfolk, from where he travelled west recording his thoughts, observations and poetical musings, many of which were unhappy, before reaching Ivinghoe Beacon. Thomas died in action in 1917 at Arras on the Western Front.

Robert Macfarlane has followed in Thomas's footsteps, and his observations form a chapter in his book *The Old Ways* (2012), which traces these ancient routes across England.

John Clare (1793–1864)

> *Inclosurecame and trampled on the grave*
>
> *Of labour's rights and left the poor a slave*
>
> *And birds and trees and flowers without a name*
>
> *All sighed when lawless law's enclosure came.*

('The Mores', 1832)

John Clare[12] is not directly connected to Bedfordshire; he was born and grew up in the south-east of the neighbouring county of Northamptonshire. Often known as the Peasant Poet, Clare was born in the parish of Helpston (now in Cambridgeshire), where he lived through the rural upheaval of the parliamentary enclosure movement. His poetry is important because he wrote about the radical, rapid changes that took place across lowland England during the early nineteenth century, as the drive to improve

---

[12] Clare acknowledged the influence of Robert Bloomfield (1766–1823), who was also a poet writing pastoral or rural verse. His work is based on his early life in Suffolk, but later in life he lived in the Bedfordshire town of Shefford and is buried in the churchyard at Campton. Bloomfield is best remembered for his poem, 'The Farmer's Boy'.

agricultural production swept aside the old patterns of rural life and destroyed livelihoods. Many former agricultural workers and their children moved away from the countryside to overcrowded cities, seeking factory work. The new agricultural economy required pastures to be ploughed up, trees to be uprooted, fens to be drained, common land to be privatised, and newly enclosed fields to be bounded by regular hedges. The parish of Helpston was enclosed in 1809, and Clare witnessed the plight of the displaced and disadvantaged. Coming from a poor family with his father earning a precarious living as a day labourer, the social upheaval had a direct and profound effect on Clare as a young man. He compares the damage of enclosure as akin to the action in Europe of Napoleon Bonaparte – which was strong, topical stuff in the midst of England's war with France. The political tone of his verse is captured by lines such as:

> A board sticks up to notice 'no road here'
>
> And on the tree with ivy overhung
>
> The hated sign by vulgar taste is hung
>
> As tho' the very birds should learn to know
>
> When they go there they must no further go
>
> Thus, with the poor, scared freedom bade goodbye
>
> And much they feel it in the smothered sigh.

('The Mores', 1832)

In later life, Clare suffered from bouts of mental illness and was sent to a private asylum in Essex, close to Epping Forest. In July 1841 he absconded and walked back to his home in Northamptonshire along the route of the York road, now the A1. In his journal, he records this walk of 'eighty lame and limping miles in four haunted, hungry days', describing the land and places in Bedfordshire he passed through – or avoided.

John Clare: twenty coy bumbarrels in a drove

After his death, John Clare's poetry faded from popular appreciation. However, there was a revival of interest in his work in the late twentieth century, which was all the more remarkable, given that much of the countryside he described has vanished. Moreover, his language is peppered with words that are no longer in use, even in rural areas. His appeal to the urban English reader is sometimes compared to that of Robert Burns in Scotland, whose dialect is also difficult for many modern readers to understand. Today, Clare is recognised as an important poet, whose work gives a compelling glimpse of rural England in the nineteenth century. In 1996, his poem, 'Emmonsail's Heath in Winter', was ranked fifty-first in *The Nation's Favourite Poems* (BBC Books).

The countryside he describes swarmed with life. Clare writes of birds, some long since disappeared from the countryside: corncrakes called from among the crops, ravens nested in ancient oaks, and nightjars circled the heathland.

'Emmonsail's Heath in Winter'

I love to see the old heath's withered brake

Mingle its crumpled leaves with furze and ling,

While the old heron from the lonely lake

Starts slow and flaps its melancholy wing,

An oddling crow in idle motion swing

On the half rotten ash tree's topmost twig,

Beside whose trunk the gypsy makes his bed.

Up flies the bouncing woodcock from the brig

Where a black quagmire quakes beneath the tread;

The fieldfares chatter in the whistling thorn

And for the haw round fields and closen rove,

And coy bumbarrels, twenty in a drove,

Flit down the hedgerows in the frozen plain

And hang on little twigs and start again.

(A brake is a thicket; a bumbarrel is a long-tailed tit; Emmonsail's Heath is now arable farmland near Helpston, where Clare was born in 1793.)

CHAPTER 13
THE POWER OF PLACE – MORE THAN JUST A NICE VIEW

My intention, in writing this book, was to describe how local people, influenced by national events, have changed the countryside in one part of lowland England. I wanted to keep people at the heart of the book, and to trace the part played by individuals and institutions on the appearance of the countryside we see today. A few of these people are historical figures, such as Capability Brown, who imprinted his characteristic landscape features on the parklands along the Greensand Ridge. Others are less well known, such as the Bedfordshire agricultural machinery inventors, and the Laxton family of fruit nurserymen.

Throughout the historical account, the challenge has been to provide insights into how national events and trends have impacted on the pattern of landscape use and change in Bedfordshire. A local interest in the county should make the story more compelling and immediate. So, while we may be aware from history books of the parliamentary enclosures of the eighteenth century, understanding that this led directly to the pattern of regular and geometric fields we see today in Bedfordshire gives us an insight into the history of the familiar landscape we see today and should enhance any walk or ramble. Furthermore, the central role played by local people, dukes and tenants, brick-makers and market gardeners, foresters and conservationists in the past gives a local background to the national story.

My first book, *An Unassuming County: The Making of the Bedfordshire Countryside,* emphasises the physical attributes of the landscape – the geology, the soil cover, and the pattern of agricultural land use. This second book takes the story beyond the natural framework and shows how the basic physical structure of the land has been both altered and managed by determined and far-sighted individuals to create productive, attractive landscapes. This has required ambition and vision, energy – and astounding amounts of money. This commitment has mastered the underlying physical limitations of the land and moulded it to suit an ideal, or perhaps a fashion. An example is the work of Capability Brown. When creating his signature water features he understood that the Greensand rocks act as an aquifer, and the resulting springs along the base of the outcrop could be channelled to fill ponds in Ampthill Park and elsewhere. These water features were valued by his clients, since the fashion at the time was for water to be an essential landscape element. The ideal was for the house to be mirrored in an artificial pond, or lake.

The pragmatic, practical monks of the thirteenth century, supported by the great religious orders, moved into the relatively empty areas along the Greensand Ridge. Here they developed land and grazed sheep, hence giving an impression – at least to their benefactors – of clearing wilderness and living in solitude. This remoteness was seen as an important part of monastic life. Their handiwork is still evident to walkers along the Greensand Ridge footpath today, with fishponds at Warden and extensive woodlands at Chicksands.

The story of any landscape is therefore also a story of human relationships, patterns of trade, religion, fashion, warfare and politics, mixed up with technological advances in agriculture. It is not a linear story: rather, the history has branches and strands that part and then merge. The influence of climate on agriculture and land has also been a consistent theme throughout this book, and it would be foolish to assume this to be only a historical artefact. A glance at the rise in average temperatures since 1850 should be enough to prompt questions about what we will do in future: will the crops we grow now still be suitable in future? What will be the likely impact of climate change on yields? Will new pests or other threats be imported? How adaptable are we as land users?

A recurring theme in this book has been the increasing pace of change that affects the countryside. This will not only continue, but will also accelerate further as the human ability to achieve transformation becomes cheaper and more widely available. A hedgerow that would have taken months to plant during enclosure, and decades more to mature, can disappear in a day. The speed and frequency of change is now much more sudden, unpredictable and far-reaching. This requires us to ask fundamental questions, such as: what do we – as residents, visitors, farmers or conservationists – expect from rural England? As always, these changes can be viewed as a threat or an opportunity. As in the past, today the countryside is not always calm and peaceful, but can become contested terrain.

Debate around the future of the countryside has been with us since John Clare protested against the enclosures. The UK's 2016 decision to leave the European Union has the potential to be a catalyst for huge change in the countryside. Few industries will be impacted in a more direct way than farming – and the half a million people employed in the industry. However, at the time of writing there is no agreed consensus on a way forward.

Currently, the UK receives around £3 billion each year from the European farming subsidy – what will replace that after the UK has left the EU? This sum is roughly equal to the cost of a new aircraft carrier (minus the planes). On leaving the EU, agriculture in the UK will need to find substantial funds to continue operating, and this funding has been underwritten by the government until the end of the next parliament. So what is the taxpayer paying for exactly, and is there agreement on the amount and destination of the funds? The government consultation paper (Defra, 2018) argues that this is an opportunity for 'fundamental reform', and warns that the scope of the changes is wide and ambitious. Farmers are to be incentivised to create new habitats, increase biodiversity, reduce flooding, mitigate climate change, and improve air quality. Public money is to be spent on 'public goods' – which include restoring peat bogs and maintaining dry stone walls in the countryside.

Therefore, the question becomes: are subsidies about food security, flood protection, conserving ancient woods, improving access to the countryside, or support for the social fabric of rural Britain? It is inevitable that in future when this amount of funding appears in the national accounts there will be a lively debate on how best the money can be spent.

Agricultural stewardship agreements funded by Europe have helped to achieve modest gains in the protection of wildlife.[13] So, will this continue? Does the public want to fund such interventions? We could see what has been called a democratisation of the

---

[13] Research into numbers of farmland birds over a 30-year period disputes this interpretation of improvement, however. Bird numbers across the EU member states have more than halved in the past 30 years, with France suffering the largest decline (Birdlife Europe, 2018).

countryside with greater public involvement, engagement and access. On the other hand, commercial farming will need continued support from the Exchequer as importing food becomes more expensive and food security again becomes paramount. Conservation and the management of land for wildlife and public enjoyment could then be pushed to the margins.

Whatever the outcome, some will argue that the provision of public funds requires a visible public benefit. One point is clear, however: keeping farms active and farmers supported in a rural economy will be critical in any efforts to protect the countryside. This will require a subsidy in many parts of Britain; the shape or form in which this will be delivered is not yet clear. A balance must be found between the farmer as a countryside steward and as a food producer. At present, the UK produces around 50 per cent of the food it needs. However, the argument for producing more goes beyond simply the supply of food to embrace the traceability of what we eat. Also important are food miles, animal welfare regulations, and the security of some three and half million jobs across the food sector.

It is sobering to realise that the Environment Agency and its devolved agencies have recorded at least one serious pollution incident from farms every week, on average, since 2010. Behind this statistic are some interesting figures: farms are getting bigger. Family farms are growing rarer. Over the decade to 2010 the number of farms fell by around 6 per cent, and the size of the average farm grew by approximately the same amount. The Black Death saw the first spike in farm size – farms grew from around 30 acres in the thirteenth century to 120 acres in the seventeenth century, due partly to a lack of people to farm the land, and a growing realisation that small farms were not efficient. Now in the twenty-first century, over 900 acres is average. Farms need many fewer employees, thanks to technology, including sophisticated machinery.

Faced with these political and social challenges, arguments over the amount of land for building development, the scale of home-grown food production, space for wind and solar farms, outlets for leisure and recreation, and the amount of land to be protected or conserved for wildlife are likely to become more urgent, and will be made at both an economic and an emotional level.

In Chapter 11 we saw how, after Second World War, pioneering legislation led to the creation of the first National Parks. Behind this bold move was the simple idea, understood by the government, that there was a 'Public Interest' in the use of land. Rather than use the contested word 'planning', the government understood that there was, and remains, a 'public interest' in how land is used.

Since the 1950s we have seen improved protection for the countryside. This reached the highest level in 2000 with the passing of the Countryside and Rights of Way Act. This legislation was opposed, as was the trespass movement in the 1930s. This shows there are real divisions over the use of land. Passions and arguments are as common as rivers and streams in pastoral England. People care about the landscape, and this book argues that we need to understand more about what is of value, why it is of value, and who places this value on the countryside. These discussions begin locally and ripple outwards, and lie at the centre of the book.

In the private sphere, there is evidence that, despite the majority of the population now being urban, there is no lack of affinity for the countryside, or land, or rural life. With nine out of ten people now living in an urban setting, there is an inevitable loosening of direct ties to the land – but there is also evidence that people continue to draw on their connection to the land and value its history. The demand for smallholdings and allotments has never been higher. From the growth in television programmes about the countryside, to memberships of conservation bodies such as the National Trust, there is ample evidence of increased interest in the natural world. Books with a countryside theme, such as Robert Macfarlane's description of ancient trackways (*The Old Ways*), link a love of the countryside to the growth of walking and ramblers groups. Even *Country Life* magazine, previously the preserve of the country house owner, is enjoying better sales. There is also an renewed interest in explaining, interpreting and understanding the countryside: the Sill National Landscape Discovery Centre recently opened in Northumberland explains the underlying geological elements that have shaped the present-day view of Hadrian's Wall. People want to be actively involved in conservation volunteering, and to learn rural skills such as hedge laying and coppicing.

A clear demonstration of public feelings to a perceived loss of countryside access was the reaction to the government's 2011 proposal to privatise the majority of government-owned forestry land. A well-organised national campaign which pointed out that such a measure would inevitably limit public access led to the government backing away from the idea – and Chancellor George Osborne's admission in the House of Commons that this had been badly judged and would not be tried again. At the local level, well-intentioned changes caused by judicious tree-cutting in Ampthill Park – intended to open up lost views once crafted by Capability Brown – led to a public debate before being accepted as a positive landscape gain.

Debate on the future of the countryside is fuelled by the seemingly unstoppable rise of land prices, the clamour for improved infrastructure and housing (especially in southern England), and the stripping out of local government as the guardian of the Public Interest through planning regulations. While these are national issues, they are inevitably focused on at a local level. In Scotland, it could be plans for re-wilding, or in Somerset, the reintroduction of beavers. In Bedfordshire, arguments are often around building on green belts, or the lack of funds to combat fly tipping. The main developmental threat is usually seen as land lost to housing, roads and warehousing units close to motorways and arterial roads. But, where to build? As Peter Hetherington points out in his thought-provoking book, *Whose Land is Our Land?* (2015), the debate can be full of contradictions. When people were recently asked to estimate the area of land in England that is presently urban, guesses ranged from a half to a quarter of all land. The actual answer is that in England, about 12 per cent is urban, with only 5 per cent covered in houses. The general perception that the countryside is disappearing is informed by the use of phrases such as 'living in a crowded island' and references to the countryside being 'concreted over'. There is often confusion over the terminology used – builders like to use the term 'greenfield sites' for new development areas which require land not previously built on, not to be confused with 'green belt', now a tattered remnant around most towns and cities. The planners would like development on brownfield sites – of which the new housing on the former brickworks sites in Bedfordshire is a great example. This is, of course, usually more expensive, as the land needs rehabilitation – and, despite builders' efforts to beautify the landscape, relics of the industrial past are often stubborn and difficult to shift.

Land prices have a real impact on these development arguments. When Milton Keynes was being built in the 1960s, each plot of land without any services cost around 1 per cent of the finished house price. Today the cost of land can be a third or more of the price of each housing unit. Patrick Collinson in the *Guardian* estimated that landowners earned £9 billion in profits from land sales in 2014–15 (Collinson, 2017).

In recent years, almost every village in Bedfordshire has experienced a housing boom, ranging from small developments of a few expensive houses, often on infilling sites, to large developments tacked onto the edge of a village. Smaller towns across Bedfordshire have expanded, with housing estates often consisting of 500 houses or more blurring the edges of the settlement and bleeding into neighbouring villages. Leighton Buzzard has gone from a population of 35,000 in 1999 to almost 50,000 today. Bedford has expanded along the A421 corridor and across the Great Ouse Valley. London and the area within the M25 has generated a seemingly unstoppable pull, and this has changed the landscape of the surrounding counties forever. This has led to frequent press reports of new towns, villages or even garden cities in the county, rekindled by support for a developmental growth corridor through Bedfordshire linking Cambridge, Milton Keynes and Oxford. This would mean Bedfordshire would be supported by new infrastructure such as restored rail links, improved roads, and thousands of new homes.

The Council for the Protection of Rural England takes these changes seriously and lobbies tirelessly for preserving green belts and urging the use of brownfield land. Despite public concern, the UK Office of National Statistics estimates that only about 3 per cent of land has legal protection in some form – that is, as a National Park, nature reserve or SSSI. A 2010 report, 'Making Space for Nature', made a plea for more, and better, conservation. The author Sir John Lawton makes his case well:

'There is compelling evidence that England's collection of wildlife sites are generally too small and too isolated, leading to decline in many of England's characteristic species. With climate change, the situation is likely to get worse. This is bad news for wildlife but also bad news for us, because the damage to nature also means

our natural environment is less able to provide the many services upon which we depend. We need more space for nature.'

The common thread running through these debates over the future of the countryside is the idea of a landscape under threat. However, it would be unfortunate to end this book without a reference to recent – and ongoing – positive changes in Bedfordshire. The 2017 launch of the Greensand Country Landscape Partnership (GCLP) gave positive recognition to a swath of elevated topography along the length of the Greensand Ridge. The most encouraging aspect of this initiative is that local people have been involved from the outset.

Funding from the Heritage Lottery Fund (HLF) has only been realised after much effort and time from a growing band of volunteers and groups such as the RSPB and the Wildlife Trusts, which exist because people care enough to pay subscriptions and give of their time. These voluntary efforts are repeated across Bedfordshire and nationally, thanks to government cuts in funding. This new Landscape Partnership in Bedfordshire has the potential to stabilise areas of landscape under pressure and offers a real opportunity for people to become more engaged with the countryside. Hopefully, this will also leave a legacy of organised local groups which can carry on making the case for conservation. Figure 13.1 shows some members of the local group at Old Warden.

At the centre of this book is the contention that many people retain an active interest in the countryside and that an accessible book about how the landscape in this part of England has evolved will be useful. Ultimately, we are the stewards of the countryside – and the challenge is, at minimum, to do no harm. It would be false to claim that Bedfordshire has a unique or spectacular landscape. Much of the land we walk in today is typical of large tracts of the south Midlands, thanks mainly to a shared geological history. However, there are fine examples of a number of landscape types which are worth conserving and protecting – such as the fine parklands of the Greensand Country, with their excellent walking, and the sandy heaths along the same belt of sandstone rock. Chalk grasslands in the south of the county with their unique collections of orchids and rare butterflies – and superb views – provide opportunities for recreation, and there are smaller

Figure 13.1. In 2017, the GCLP supported a geophysical survey of the site of the Cistercian Abbey in Warden by a professional geophysical and archaeological unit, assisted by volunteers. This work was planned and managed by the Old Warden Historical Society. Public display boards that show how the abbey may have looked in the thirteenth century will be produced using the new archaeological evidence. (This image is reproduced with permission of the Old Warden Historical Society. Photographer: Margaret Roberts.

fragments of meadow grasslands to lift the spirits with wildflowersin spring, and ancient woodlands full of bluebells. Otters have returned to our rivers, and red kites and buzzards are common sights in the sky over Bedfordshire. The county therefore has a great variety of landscapes in a compact area, making space for orchids and rare butterflies.

Therefore the task is to agree what is worth protecting – if necessary, we must argue to stop the erosion of our most valued landscapes, and to ensure that public access to them is not made more difficult. However we cannot preserve everything. Conservation can only be achieved by fostering an increased level of public engagement and some understanding of how our landscape came to be as it is today. That is what landscape history is all about.

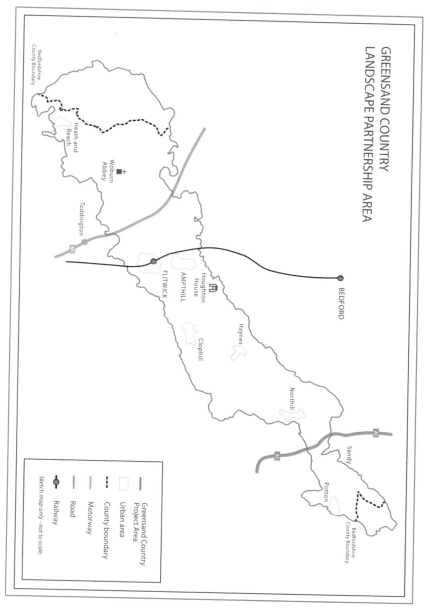

Figure 13.2.

THE GREENSAND COUNTRY LANDSCAPE PARTNERSHIP will operate within the area shown, which is bounded by the Greensand geology in Bedfordshire, with small areas in adjacent counties. This work is supported by the Heritage Lottery Fund. (Drawn by John Hambley from GCLP documentary material.)

The Greensand Country Landscape Partnership

A recent initiative, which combines the ethos of conservation with public involvement, is a national programme funded by the Heritage Lottery Fund. The aim is to encourage the creation of landscape partnerships throughout the UK. The aim of these partnerships is 'to better protect and conserve specific areas of countryside'. This is a bold attempt to extend the level of recognition for valued and distinctive parts of the landscape beyond the iconic National Parks, and at the same time promote public access without compromising the existing sustainable use of the land for agriculture or forestry. This is where the word 'partnership' is important: these agencies aspire to be as far-reaching as possible and to include rural business representatives, farming and wildlife organisations, local conservation groups, recreational countryside users such as ramblers, cyclists and horse riders, and local government from parish level upwards.

In Bedfordshire a group of like-minded people and organisations has been working to create such a Landscape Partnership for an area of the Greensand Ridge, along which the 44-mile long-distance footpath known as the Greensand Ridge Walk extends. The challenge for the initial group bidding for HLF funding has been to describe this area of landscape and identify what makes it unique. Technical studies launched to support this application have included a Landscape Character Assessment to capture the essence of what is now described as the Greensand Country.

This area, illustrated in Figure 13.2, is an important recreational outlet for the small towns and larger communities in Bedfordshire and Buckinghamshire and is also much loved and visited by local residents. This is a working landscape of farms and plantation forestry, as well as the home of many small businesses. It also supports a modest tourist trade. The Greensand Country is characterised by a great variety of landscapes in a compact area. A former quarry industry has largely been replaced by managed areas of forestry, heath and parkland, and there are fragments of ancient woodlands that are alive with bluebells in the spring. The past land uses of market gardens, rabbit warrens, royal hunting reserves, fish ponds, abbeys and monasteries are important features of this countryside and add interest for the visitor. This is now the country of red kites, buzzards, badgers and adders, where irregular hedged fields offer views across the more geometric arable landscapes of the Bedfordshire clay vales. The Greensand Ridge Walk crosses extensive parkland dotted with mature and often exotic trees, dips into the major river valleys, and leads the walker across wildflower meadows. A country pub is never far away.

APPENDIX: PLACES TO VISIT

This book is essentially about geography. Many of the places mentioned in the text are accessible to the public, and are worth visiting as they are examples of the landscapes or countryside described in the book. The list below is not comprehensive, as this would simply become a gazetteer for Bedfordshire. Rather, a few locations are listed for each chapter, with an accompanying note about each.

Grid references

The position of each place can be determined from a grid reference using a standard Ordnance Survey (OS) 1:50,000 scale map. All OS maps contain an explanation of how to use this geographic location system. The grid lines on the map form part of the National Grid and are spaced 1 kilometre apart. To locate a point within 100 metres, use the vertical lines and read the number to the *left* of the point. This gives the first two numbers; then estimate tenths of a kilometre to the point itself. This is the 'easting'. The 'northing', which forms the next three numbers, is determined by finding the horizontal line *below* the point and then estimating tenths of a kilometre to the point required.

The letters relate to which map sheets the point is on. Bedfordshire is mostly within sheets beginning 'TL', with some western parts of the county on sheets beginning 'SP'. The best maps to use for Bedfordshire are the 1:25,000 scale Explorer Series. The sheets required are 208 (Bedford and St Neots), 191 (Buckingham and Milton Keynes) and 193 (Luton and Dunstable). A small area in the south is on sheet 182 (St Albans and Hatfield).

Chapter 1

The Higgins Bedford (www.thehigginsbedford.org.uk/) is an art gallery and museum close to the River Great Ouse in Bedford. The prehistoric galleries have excellent examples of Palaeolithic artefacts found in the area. Photographs of some of these items have been used as illustrations in the text.

The Icknield Way is a long-distance footpath. This can be joined at many places in south Bedfordshire close to Luton or Dunstable, such as at Warden Hill (OS Explorer Map 193, TL 093 260). Details of the long-distance footpath network in Bedfordshire can be found at the Long Distance Walkers Association website, www.ldwa.com.

Biddenham Pit (TL 023 504) is one of forty Sites of Special Scientific Interest (SSSIs) in Bedfordshire. The site is special because it is an example of an ancient gravel terrace of the Bedfordshire Ouse. Stone implements from the Palaeolithic era have been recovered from the lower levels of this geological terrace formation.

Chapter 2

Iron Age forts in Bedfordshire include **Mowsbury** (TL 065 533), north of Bedford, and **Galley Hill** (TL 185 478) in the RSPB reserve at Sandy . Both are accessible listed ancient monuments with clearly visible defence works. (www.rspb.org.uk/reserves-and-events/reserves-a-z/the-lodge).

Five Knolls Barrows on the outskirts of Dunstable (TL 006 209), on the edge of the Dunstable Downs, are on land managed by the National Trust. The seven barrows are characteristic of Bronze Age burials, but in fact span a long period, from 2000–700 BC. This site is also a listed ancient monument.

Chapter 3

Roman discoveries from Sandy can be viewed at the town council offices on Cambridge Road (01767-681491, admin@sandytowncouncil.gov.uk). Photographs and artefacts uncovered during excavations at the town's cemetery are on display.

A mosaic floor from a Roman villa at Bancroft is mounted on a wall in the Milton Keynes shopping centre, The Centre: MK. The main rooms in the villa complex have been marked out at Bancroft Park (SP 827 405). and a fish pond has been reconstructed there. The villa was reburied after excavation and is no longer visible above ground.

Chapter 4

Saxon churches in Bedfordshire include those at Turvey, Stevington and Carlton in the north and St Peter's in Bedford.

Yttingaford (Peace Meadow) (SP 916 245), by the River Ouzel close to Leighton Buzzard, is the site where an agreement was reached in AD 906 between the Danish settlers to the east and the Saxon kingdoms to the west. The site is in Tiddenfoot Waterside Park (www.tiddenfoot.org.uk).

Chapter 5

Cainhoe Castle, Clophill (TL 098 374), is a good example of a Norman motte with extensive baileys set on a strategic site close to the River Flit. There is also the castle mound in Bedford and smaller mottes at Teddington, Flitwick, Pirton and Yelden in north Bedfordshire. Access to Cainhoe is by a footpath heading south from Clophill High Street.

Glebe Meadows at Houghton Conquest (TL 045 4030) are a surviving relic of mediaeval ridge and furrow ploughing. Other examples in Bedfordshire are more difficult to view as they are on private land.

Warden Abbey and its fish ponds are located at TL I22 438. However, the site is on private property with no public access. The nearby Warden Vineyard (ww.wardenvineyard.org.uk/) is on the former Abbey estate and is open to the public a few times each year.

Stotfold Water Mill is a restored water mill which is occasionally open to the public. Opening times can be checked at www.stotfoldmill.com. The Domesday Book records four mills in this area, one of which is certain to be the surviving mill.

Chapter 6

Ruxox Farm (TL 047 359) is one of over 6000 moated sites in England. This location is a good example of continuity of settlement, with Roman finds adjacent to an area enclosed by wide ditches which fill with water in wet periods. The moat was probably constructed during the early fourteenth century.

Sharnbrook Moat (SP 989 595) is now in a small nature reserve. Often referred to as Sharnbrook Castle, this earthwork is best described as a moated site typical of many examples throughout Bedfordshire.

Chapter 7

Old Warden (TL 035 437) is an example of a 1820s remodelled village constructed by the 3rd Baron Ongley to fit within a designed landscape. This style of rural building is often described as rustic or cottage orné.

Ampthill Great Park (TL 035 384) has many of the signature features of a landscape designed by Capability Brown. These include prominent clumps of trees set as 'eye-catchers', a pond, which is a relic of a much larger water feature, a carriage drive flanked by trees, and parkland walks. The Park is free and open to the public.

Wrest Park at Silsoe

(www.english-heritage.org.uk/visit/places/wrest-park) is an English Heritage site which provides examples of differing periods of garden history and design. The park has one of the few surviving examples of an early eighteenth-century formal garden, and includes some later Capability Brown features.

Woburn Abbey (www.woburnabbey.co.uk/) is the best example in Bedfordshire of Humphry Repton's influence on a parkland landscape. The house and gardens are open to the public and guided tours of the gardens are often offered. The parkland is crossed by many footpaths which are rights of way and provide splendid views of the landscaped estate.

Flitwick Manor Park (TL 036 344) is open to the public throughout the year, free of charge. It contains many exotic trees that were brought to the UK and planted in the late eighteenth and early nineteenth century.

Chapter 8

A model of the **Howard Champion Plough** is on display at The Higgins Bedford, along with other items that trace Bedfordshire's links to agricultural engineering.

Chapter 9

Marston Vale Millennium Country Park (www.marstonvale.org/) was created on the site of former brick pits south of Bedford. This public area is now landscaped and includes a bird reserve and observation hides, a water sports centre, marked footpaths and cycle routes. The park is free and open during daylight hours.

Chapter 10

Wrest Park, Silsoe, was utilised in the Great War as a hospital, and later as a convalescent home for soldiers. The building and gardens are now owned by English Heritage and there are periodic exhibitions at the site which illustrate the wartime history of the house.

Chapter 11

Marl Lakes and Nature Reserve at Houghton Regis (TL 008 235) is a former chalk quarry. There are many such examples in Bedfordshire.

Chapter 12

The Bunyan oak tree at Harlington (TL 045 314) is a good place to begin the long-distance Bunyan Trail which winds through much of Bedfordshire. This route gives access to many of the villages associated with John Bunyan and is described on the Long-Distance Walkers Association website, www.ldwa.com.

Houghton House (TL 02894) is now a romantic ruin. It was painted by Edward Callam as part of his Bunyan suite of paintings. This house was to Bunyan the 'house beautiful' in *The Pilgrim's Progress*.

Chapter 13

The Clophill Eco-Centre (TL 093 388) provides facilities for walkers on the Greensand Ridge Walk (described on www.ldwa.com). This centre is also the hub for numerous outdoor community and education activities.

REFERENCES

Books and other documents mentioned in the text are listed below as References. The Further Reading section is designed to encourage anyone who is interested to explore the subject more widely.

Agriculture and land classification

C.E. Fitchett, 1943, *The Land of Britain. The Report of the Land Utilisation Survey of Britain. Part 55. Bedfordshire.* Edited by Dudley Stamp. (This complements the publication in 1937 of the '1 inch to 1 mile' scale maps for the county.)

Dudley Stamp, 1948, *The Land of Britain: Its Use and Misuse,* Longman.

Agricultural history

Shimon Applebaum, 1958, 'Agriculture in Roman Britain', *British Agricultural History* 6, 2.

F. Beavington, 1975, 'The development of market gardening in Bedfordshire, 1700–1939,' *Agricultural History Review*, 23, 1.

Thomas Batchelor, 1808 (2nd edition 1813), *A General View of the Agriculture of the County of Bedford.* Drawn up for the Board of Agriculture and published in London by B. McMillan for Richard Phelps. Reproduced by Nabu Public Domain Reprints.

Margaret Roberts, 2017, *The Original Warden Pear*, Eventispress.

Thomas Stone, 1794, *A General View of the Agriculture of the County of Bedford: With observations on the means of its improvement.* Drawn up for the Board of Agriculture.

Archaeology

Atlas of Hillforts of Britain and Ireland. Available at https://hillforts.arch.ox.ac.uk/

M. Luke, 2011, *Life in the Loop*, Albion Archaeology.

M. Luke, 2016, *Close to the Loop*, Albion Archaeology.

Bedfordshire history

Peter Bigmore, 1979, *The Bedfordshire and Huntingdonshire Landscape*, Hodder & Stoughton.

Simon Houfe, 1995, *Bedfordshire*, Pimlico County History Guide.

Extraction industries

Cox, 1979, 'Brick-making: A History and Gazetteer', Bedfordshire County Council.

Richard Hillier, 1981, *Clay that Burns: A history of the Fletton brick industry*, London Brick Company.

Forestry and woodland

John Evelyn, 1664, S*ylva – A Discourse of Forest Trees and the Propagation of Timber*. Reprinted by Forgotten Books, 2017.

Herman Porter, republished June 2017, *The 126 Company Canadian Forestry Corps, Ampthill, 1917–18. Large-scale felling and dressing of timber before shipping to Europe in the Great War for use in the trenches and below surface fortifications*, Ampthill and District Archaeological & Local History Society.

Gardens

Andrew Hann and Shelley Garland, 2011, *Wrest Park, En*glish Heritage.

J.C. Louden, 1840, *The Landscape Gardening and Architecture of the Late Humphry Repton,* Cambridge University Press.

Geology

Bernard O'Connor, 1998, *The Dinosaurs on Sandy Heath*, self-published.

Bernard O'Connor (n.d.), *The Shillington Fossil Diggings*, self-published.

Irish history

Garrett Carr, 2017, *The Rule of the Land: Walking Ireland's Border*. Faber & Faber.

Local history

Joyce Godber, 1984, *History of Bedfordshire*. Bedfordshire County Council.

Landscape history

Jane Brown, 2011, *Lancelot 'Capability' Brown, 1917–1973: The Omnipotent Magician*, Vintage Digital.

W.G. Hoskins, 1955, 1967, *The Making of the English Landscape*, Hodder & Stoughton.

Brian Kerr, 2014, *An Unassuming County: The Making of the Bedfordshire Countryside*, Eventispress.

John Phibbs. *'Ampthill Park: an illustrated guide.'* 2016 reprint of an earlier booklet. Available from Ampthill Town Council offices.

Soils

George Sinclair, 1816, *Hortus Gramineus Woburnensis*. From a plant catalogue by James Forbes, 1833. (Third edition published 1826.)

Topography

David Alderman and Pamela Stevenson, 1993, *Champion Trees of Bedfordshire*, Bedfordshire County Council (out of print).

A.J. Foster, 1901, *Bunyan's Country: Studies in the Bedfordshire Topography of the Pilgrim's Progress*, H. Virtue & Company, London. (Available in facsimile form from Trieste Publishing, www.triestepublishing.com.)

Charles Hooper, 1928, *The Bunyan Country*, Cecil Palmer, London.

Miscellaneous

Daniel Defoe, 1978 (reprinted), *A Tour through the Whole Island of Great Britain*, Penguin Classics.

Edward Thomas, 1913, *The Icknield Way*, Constable & Co.

George Deaux, 1969, *The Black Death 1347*, David McKay & Co.

HMSO, 1966, 'Leisure and the Countryside: England and Wales'.

Peter Hetherington, 2015, *Whose Land is Our Land? The Use and Abuse of Britain's Forgotten Acres*, Policy Press Insights.

Robert Macfarlane, 2012, *The Old Ways*, Hamish Hamilton.

Roger Fisher, 1763, *Heart of Oak, the British Bulwark* (reprinted in 2018 by Forgotten Books).

Sir John Lawton, 2010, 'Making Space for Nature: A review of England's wildlife sites'. Available at https://www.gov.uk/government/news/making-space-for-nature-a-review-of-englands-wildlife-sites-published-today

Patrick Collinson, 2917, 'House prices aren't the issue – land prices are', *Guardian*, 18 November. Available at: https://www.theguardian.com/money/blog/2017/nov/18/house-prices-land-prices-cheaper-homes

FURTHER READING

Agricultural Land Classification of England and Wales, 1969, 'A report to accompany Sheet 147, Luton & Bedford' (accompanied by a map at 1: 63,360).

T.W. Beastall, 1978, 'Agricultural Revolution in Lincolnshire,' published by the History of Lincolnshire Committee.

R.I. Bradley and P.S. Wright, 1988, Soils of the Shuttleworth Estate, Biggleswade, Bedfordshire, Cranfield University.

British Geological Survey and Department of the Environment, 1995, 'Bedfordshire: A Summary of Mineral Resource Information for Development Plans'. Scale 1:100,000.

Betty Chambers, 1983, Thomas Jefferys and his Map of Bedfordshire, Bedfordshire Historical Society.

Peter Clarke, 2011, East Bedfordshire's Arcadia: History or prophecy? Market gardening yesterday or tomorrow. 1969–2009, Nottingham Square.

Geoffrey Cowley, 1972, County Review: Minerals Aspect Report, Bedfordshire County Council.

Mike Dawson, n.d., Roman Sandy, Bedfordshire County Archaeology Service. Publication sponsored by Redlands Aggregates.

Department for the Environment, Food and Rural Affairs (Defra), 2018, Health and Harmony: the future for food, farming, and environment in a Green Brexit. Available at: https://www.gov.uk/government/consultations/the-future-for-food-farming-and-the-environment

Peter Dewey, 2008, Iron Harvests of the Field: the Making of Farm Machinery in Britain since 1800, Carnegie Publishing.

Timothy Farewell, Peter Friend, Martin Whiteley and Joanna Zawadzka, 2011, The Mapping of Landscapes, Geology and Soils in Bedfordshire and Cambridgeshire, Bedfordshire Geology Group.

C.G. Harper, 1928, The Bunyan Country, Cecil Palmer, London.

Christine Hill, 2014, *Old Warden: Tales of Tenants & Squires*, Amberley Press.

Kathy Hindle and Lee Irvine, 1990, *A Thoroughly Good Fellow. The Story of Dan Albone, Inventor and Cyclist*, Bedfordshire County Council.

C.A.H. Hodge et al., 1984, *Soils and their Use in Eastern England*, Soil Survey of England and Wales.

W.G. Hoskins, 1973, *English Landscapes*, BBC Publications.

D. Kennett, 1978, *A Portrait of Bedfordshire*, Robert Hale.

D.W. King, 1969, *Soils of the Luton and Bedford District. A Reconnaissance Survey. Special Survey No. 1*, Soil Survey of England & Wales, 1969. (This contains a black-and-white map at the scale of 1 inch to 1 mile.)

Robert Lacey and Danny Danziger, 1999, *The Year 1000: What life was like at the turn of the first millennium*. Little, Brown.

B.K. Lambert and A. Gotti, 2012, *The Good Gardens Guide*, Reader's Digest.

G.D. Nicholls, 1947, 'Introduction to the geology of Bedfordshire,' *Journal of the Bedfordshire Natural History Society and Field Club*, 2, 9–16. Contains a black-and-white geology map.

D. Niemann, 2016, *A Tale of Trees*, London.

North Hertfordshire Museum, January 2017, 'How Old is the Icknield Way?' Blog post. Available at: http://www.northhertsmuseum.org/north-herts-museum-update-how-old-is-the-icknield-way/

Martin Oake et al., 2007, *Research and Archaeology: Resource Assessment, Research Agenda and Strategy. Bedfordshire Archaeology* Monograph 9, Bedfordshire County Council and The Bedfordshire Archaeology Council.

Mary Phillips, 1988. *The Clophill Story,* self-published.

Francis Pryor, 2010, *The Making of the British Landscape*, Penguin Books.

Oliver Rackham, 1976, *Trees and Woodland in the British Landscape*, J.M. Dent & Sons.

Oliver Rackham, 1980, *Ancient Woodland: Its History, Vegetation and Uses in England,* Edward Arnold.

Oliver Rackham, 1986, *The History of the Countryside*, J.M. Dent & Sons.

T. Rigg, 1916, 'The soils and crops of the market garden district of Biggleswade,' *Journal of Agricultural Science*, VII, IV. (Unfortunately, only includes very small-scale maps.)

Frank Stenton, 2001, *Anglo-Saxon England*, 3rd edn, Oxford University Press.

The Bedford and Luton Regionally Important Geological and Geomorphological Sites (RIDS) Group, and Jill Eyers, n.d., *The Building Stones of Bedfordshire*, Bedfordshire and Luton Geology Group.

The Federation of Bedfordshire Women's Institutes, 1988, *The Bedfordshire Village Book*.

Ann Williams and G.H. Martin (eds), 1992, *Domesday Book: A Complete Translation*, Penguin Books (see pp. 562–588).

John Wright, 2017, *A Natural History of the Hedgerow*, Profile.

P.S. Wright, 1987, Soils of Bedfordshire 1. Soil Record 112 (Sheet TL 14, Biggleswade). (Also contains a 1:25,000 map.)

INDEX

All locations mentioned in the text are marked on a page figure at the end of the Preface. Subjects which are mentioned in a Box are marked in **bold**, and *italics* indicate that the topic is also represented by an image